The Corridors of Time · VII ·

MERCHANT VENTURERS IN BRONZE

By HAROLD PEAKE and
HERBERT JOHN FLEURE

NEW HAVEN · YALE UNIVERSITY PRESS
LONDON · HUMPHREY MILFORD
OXFORD UNIVERSITY PRESS
1931

PRINTED IN GREAT BRITAIN AT THE UNIVERSITY PRESS, OXFORD
BY JOHN JOHNSON, PRINTER TO THE UNIVERSITY

PREFACE

OUR last volume in this series, under the title of 'The Way of the Sea', discussed a phase of civilization which, in Europe at any rate, was characterized by a remarkable development of long-distance intercourse. The west awoke to cultural relations with the civilizations of the Ægean, and foundations were laid from which have built themselves traditions and customs that linger on to our own times. The present volume deals with a phase of social evolution that is remarkably different. The old schemes of intercourse diminish in importance and some disappear, but European life is not thereby reduced to nothingness. There are, on the contrary, efforts to establish the art of metallurgy at various centres, and permanent villages and agriculture spread in Central Europe, with obvious pressure from the Russian steppe which appears to empty itself. Aryan hordes invade India, Hyksos descend on Egypt; there is evidence far and wide for a period in which there were many dry, warm summers and a pressing out of peoples from the rainless lands. In Central Europe local groups begin to take shape and to suggest, in some cases, that their descendants are the local groups of to-day, not necessarily, of course, speaking the same language; but the continued lack of an individuality in culture in Gaul at this stage is most marked. The east of that country links itself with lands farther east still, the west focuses its interest on the sea-coasts. That neither Spain nor Italy shows strong individuality is natural enough in a period of warmth and drought, but it is the age of the glory of Crete. The end of our period sees the resurgence of Egypt under the great 18th Dynasty, but it is an Egypt equipped with the horse and dreaming of vast dominion, an early edition of that Imperialistic ideal which has so disturbed the world ever since. In Egypt, in India, probably in China and in Europe there are new beginnings that in India and Europe, at least, are full of importance for modern life, and it is with an eye on the modern world and its problems that this series is being written.

The present volume surveys a period that famous specialists have made their own, and it is fitting that we should here acknowledge a general and a deep indebtedness to the work of Petrie, Déchelette,

Preface

Lissauer, Sophus Müller, Sir Arthur Evans, Childe, Reinecke, and many others.

Many thanks are due to the authors, editors, and publishers of the following works and journals for permission to reproduce figures: *Rassenkunde des deutschen Volkes*, by H. F. K. Günther (J. F. Lehmanns Verlag, München), for figs. 2c–e and 3c; *Reallexikon der Vorgeschichte*, vols. i, v, vii, viii, and xi (Walter de Gruyter & Co., Berlin), for figs. 2a and b, 3a, 19a, b, e, and f, 20b–e, 22, 25, and 27; *Troja*, by H. Schliemann (John Murray), for fig. 52; *Mycenae*, by H. Schliemann (John Murray), for figs. 50 and 51; *Délégation en Perse, Mémoires*, tome i (Librairie E. Leroux, Paris), for fig. 53; *La Sardegna*, by G. Sergi (Fratelli Bocca, Torino), for fig. 4a; *Rassen der jüngeren Steinzeit in Europa*, by W. Scheidt (J. F. Lehmanns Verlag, München), for fig. 4b; *A Guide to the Antiquities of the Bronze Age*, 2nd edition (British Museum), for fig. 5a and d; *Beth-Pelet*, vol. i, by Professor Sir Flinders Petrie (Bernard Quaritch, Ltd.), for fig. 54; *La Civilisation énéolithique dans la péninsule ibérique*, by Nils Åberg (Vilhelm Ekmans Universitetsfond, Upsala), for fig. 5b; *The Dawn of European Civilization*, by V. Gordon Childe (Kegan Paul, Trench, Trubner & Co., Ltd.), for fig. 5c; *Manuel d'archéologie préhistorique celtique et gallo-romaine*, vol. ii, by J. Déchelette (Librairie A. Picard, Paris), for fig. 6; *Bronze Age in Ireland*, by G. Coffey (Hodges, Figgis, & Co., Dublin), for fig. 7; *Bronze Age Pottery*, vol. ii, by J. Abercromby (Clarendon Press), for figs. 9 and 10; *Urgeschichte*, by Hoernes-Menghin (Anton Schroll & Co., Vienna), for fig. 24; *The Stone and Bronze Ages in Italy*, by T. E. Peet (Clarendon Press), for fig. 3; *Guide to the Collection of Irish Antiquities*, by E. C. R. Armstrong (Nat. Museum of Science and Art, Dublin), for fig. 8; *The Aegean Civilization*, by G. Glotz (Kegan Paul, Trench, Trubner & Co., Ltd.), for fig. 39; *A Catalogue of the Greek and Etruscan Vases in the British Museum*, vol. i, part i, by E. J. Forsdyke (British Museum), for figs. 38 and 43; *The Journal of the Royal Anthropological Institute*, vol. xlvi (1916), for fig. 4d; *Annual of the British School at Athens*, vol. viii, for fig. 47; *A History of Greece*, by J. B. Bury (Macmillan & Co., Ltd.), for fig. 49; *A History of Egypt*, 2nd edition, by J. H. Breasted (Scribner's Sons, New York; Hodder & Stoughton Ltd., London), for fig. 55; *Media, Babylon, and Persia*, by Z. A. Ragozin (T. Fisher Unwin Ltd. (Ernest Benn Ltd.)), for fig. 57; *Ancient Egypt*, by G. Rawlinson (T. Fisher Unwin Ltd. (Ernest Benn Ltd.)), for fig. 66, and *The Danube in Prehistory*, by V. Gordon Childe (Clarendon Press), for figs. 18, 19c, d, g, h, i, and k, 20a, and 26; *Bullettino di Paletnologia Italiana* (Museo Preistorico ed Etnografico 'Luigi Pigorini', Rome), for figs. 30 and 32.

CONTENTS

1. The Peoples of Europe. 1
2. The Early Bronze Age in Western Europe . . 13
3. Carnac and Stonehenge 29
4. The Early Bronze Age in Central Europe . . 40
5. The Early Middle Bronze Age in Central Europe . 55
6. The Middle Bronze Age in West and South-West Europe 70
7. The Aegean in the Early Bronze Age . . . 81
8. Crete and Mycenaean Greece 96
9. Trouble in the Near East 112
10. Iranians, Aryans, and Chinese 123
11. Recovery in the Near East 140
12. Chronological Summary 157

INDEX 167

LIST OF ILLUSTRATIONS

1. Map of Central Europe in the earlier phases of the Bronze Age — viii
2. Central European broad heads 5
3. *a.* Skull from Rotschloss; *b.* Skull from Ilderton, Northumberland; *c.* Central European broad head . . . 9
4. Broad-headed types from coastal regions . . . 11
5. *a.* Early metal axes; *b.* Tanged point, copper, Aljezor, S. Portugal; *c.* Tanged points, copper, Palmella; *d.* Early halberd-blade and daggers, El Oficio, Almeria, Spain . 17
6. Segmented beads and bone tubes. After Déchelette . . 20
7. Gold ornaments from Ireland. After Coffey . . . 21
8. Map showing the distribution of gold crescents . . 23
9. Four-handled jars from (*a*) Finistère; (*b*) Cornwall . . 25
10. Early British Bronze Age pottery 26
11. The spiral at New Grange. Photograph by T. H. Mason, Dublin 27

List of Illustrations

12. The Ménec alignments. Photograph by M. Z. Le Rouzic . 31
13. Plan of Stonehenge 34
14. View of Stonehenge 35
15. View of Woodhenge. Photograph kindly lent by Mrs. B. H. Cunnington 37
16. View of Ysbyty Cynfyn. Photograph by Culliford, Aberystwyth 39
17. The Area of the Aunjetitz culture 41
18. Objects of Early Metal Age. Hungary. Ingot torque and Cypriote dagger. After *Antiquity*. Upper pots Oszentiván (University Museum, Szeged); lower pots Tószeg; metal objects Csorvás (A Magyar Nemzeti Museum). Childe, *The Danube in Prehistory*, figs. 122, 124, 125 . . . 43
19. Early Aunjetitz objects. *a, b, e, f, g*, pots; *c*. amber necklace; *d*. dagger; *h, i, k*, pins. Childe, op. cit., fig. 133 and Pl. IX 44
20. Late Aunjetitz objects. *a*. Racquet-headed pin. Childe, op. cit., Plate IX; *b–e*, pots 45
21. Various types of flanged axes. *a* and *d*, Pitt-Rivers Museum, Oxford; *b*. Devizes Museum; *c*. British Museum; *e*. Peabody Museum, Harvard University, U.S.A. 47
22. Various types of bronze pins 48
23. The Lower Rhône basin in the Early Bronze Age . . 51
24. Rock engravings in the Ligurian Alps 52
25. Objects from Swiss lake villages of the phase of Les Roseaux, Morges 54
26. Early and Middle Bronze Age pots from Hungary. Childe, op. cit., figs. 146, 155, 156 f. 59
27. Early pottery of the Lausitz culture 61
28. Winged bronze axe-heads. *a*. Formerly in the Vize Collection; *b*. St. Alban's Museum; *c*. Formerly in the Rosehill Collection; *d*. Pitt-Rivers Museum, Oxford 63
29. Bronze palstaves. *a*. Pitt-Rivers Museum, Oxford; *b*. In a private collection in France; *c*. Liverpool Museum; *d*. Farnham Museum; *e*. University College of Wales, Aberystwyth; *f*. City Art Gallery, Leeds; *h*. Major H. Powell Cotton, Quex Park, Birchington; *g*. Formerly in the collection of M. Feuardent; *j*. Truro Museum; *k*. Cambridge Museum of Archaeology . 65
30. Plan of Terramara of Castellazzo. After Pigorini . . 67
31. Objects from the *Terremare* 69
32. Pottery of the First Siculan period. After Orsi, *Bull. Pal.* . 71
33. Map showing Early Bronze Age hoards in France . . 74
34. Middle Bronze Age hoards in France 76
35. The evolution of the dirk. *a*. After Boyd and Hawes; *b, c*. British Museum; *d*. Hereford Museum; *e*. Guildhall Museum; *f*. Cambridge Museum of Archaeology; *g*. London Museum . 79
36. The evolution of the spear-head in England. *a*. Ashmolean Museum, Oxford; *b, e*. British Museum; *c*. Unknown; *d*. Formerly in the Vize Collection; *f*. Taunton Museum; *g*. Warrington Museum 80
37. Plan of the Palace of Knossos. After the plan, based upon the

List of Illustrations

	results of the excavation by the late W. G. Newton and Theodore Fyfe, in Sir Arthur Evans' *The Palace of Minos at Knossos,* vol. ii, by permission of the author and Macmillan & Co., Ltd.	83
38.	Pottery imitating metal originals	84
39.	Faience plaques representing Cretan houses	85
40.	A Cretan shrine. By permission of Sir Arthur Evans	87
41.	The Phaestos disk. By permission of Sir Arthur Evans	89
42.	Gold cup from Vapheio. Photograph by E. P. Co., Athens	91
43.	High-handled vases	92
44.	Gold mask from first shaft-grave at Mycenae. Photograph by E. P. Co., Athens	95
45.	The Cup-bearer fresco. By permission of Sir Arthur Evans	97
46.	The Harvesters vase. Photograph by G. Maraghiannis, Candia	99
47.	Ivory figures of boy leapers	100
48.	The throne of Minos. Photograph by Mr. Percival Hart	103
49.	Mycenaean daggers	105
50.	The treasury of Atreus	107
51.	Shaft-graves at Mycenae	109
52.	Pottery from Hissarlik V	110
53.	Kudurru, or boundary stone, of the Kassite period	115
54.	Earthwork at Beth-pelet	119
55.	Fragment of a sitting statue of Khian	121
56.	Bronze weapons of Ahmose I. Cairo Museum	122
57.	Mortar, pestle, and strainer for Haôma. After Ragozin	125
58.	Map showing the movements of the Aryans	129
59.	Map of India showing Aryan Invasion	132
60.	Various types of Indian people. Photographs copyright by N.I.P.S.	135
61.	Early pottery of the Shang Dynasty	138
62.	Archaic inscription of the Shang Dynasty	139
63.	Amarna Letter, No. 296. Staatlichen Museum, Berlin	143
64.	Northern colonnades of Hatshepsut's temple at Der el-Bahri. Photograph by Mr. Percival Hart	145
65.	A Tell el-Amarna tablet. British Museum	151
66.	Ikhn-aton worshipping Aton	153
67.	Iron dagger from the tomb of Tutenkh-amon. Photograph by Dr. Howard Carter	156

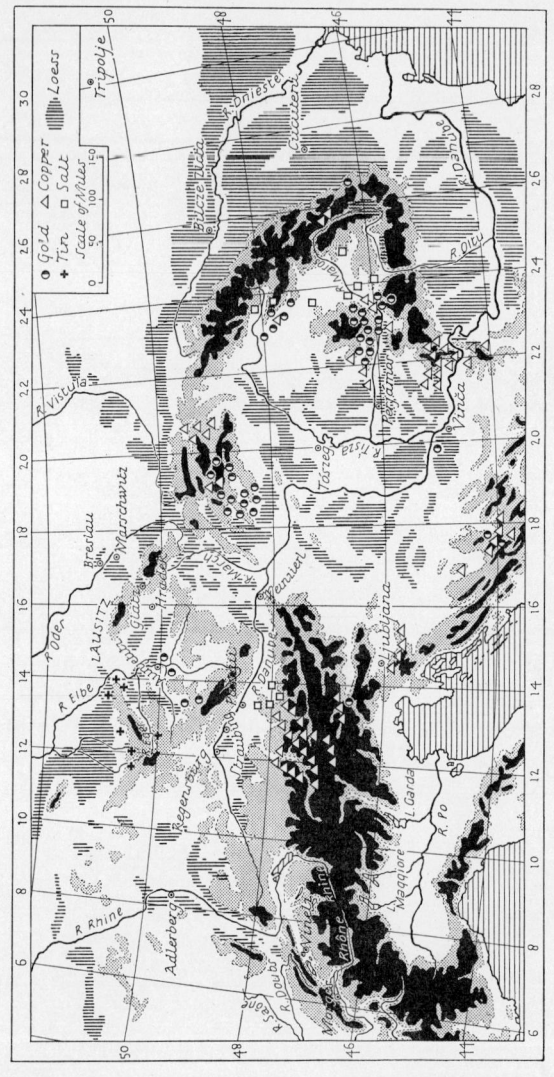

FIG. 1. Map of Central Europe in the earlier phases of the Bronze Age

I
The Peoples of Europe

WE have shown, in *The Steppe and the Sown* and *The Way of the Sea*, that there were widespread disturbances and a large development of intercourse over long distances, especially in the European region, accompanied by a great development of Aegean civilization. From that area communications spread along the Mediterranean coasts and the Atlantic coast of Europe, as well as overland through the belts of loess, the soils of which gave rise to comparatively open country where agriculture was possible. Loess, being partly wind-blown material accumulated at the foot of the hills on relatively flat land, offered little difficulty to people on the move, much of it being dry and porous. Coastwise and overland communications met at a number of centres, where the two types of culture may be found close together and to some extent overlapping; these include the Iberian peninsula, southern France, western France, Brittany, Great Britain and Ireland, the west Baltic with the adjacent parts of Holland and north Germany. Maritime influences penetrated only faintly inland, but elements of central European culture reached the sea. This occurs especially in the case of the beaker pottery, described in *The Way of the Sea*, which was also carried coastwise, along with the maritime culture, between the Iberian peninsula and Brittany.

The Way of the Sea discussed considerable exchanges of civilization in parts of central Europe among a growing and spreading peasant population, and suggested that the great city of the Troad, Hissarlik II, was concerned with this trade. That city was destroyed, apparently about 1900 B.C., and old communications suffered serious disturbance. It is noteworthy that, then, the culture associated with beaker pottery, a specialized civilization carried by a distinctive type of man, soon vanished, save for important survivals in Jutland and Britain.

Hissarlik II, and Crete as well, knew bronze about 2000 B.C., but the communications mentioned above did not at once spread that knowledge to Atlantic lands, which still for a time continued using stone and also copper and gold.

When Hissarlik II fell and communications were disturbed this was not followed by a general decay of west European culture, for that region had acquired the knowledge of grain and culture. The peasant communities that were multiplying in Europe were thus able to continue; and one notes local developments, several regions having learned the art of food production and developed a life of their own.

In each region of western Europe a background of features derived from the old intercourse formed a basis for diverse developments. Childe has suggested that early peasants in new territory formed villages to last only for a few years, until the fertility of the soil was exhausted and repairs to habitations had become urgent. A move every few years is a custom in parts of inter-tropical Africa, in a few districts in India, and also in parts of northern Korea. Such mobility makes possible exchanges in culture. Other methods of life included villages of houses built on piles laid on marshes near the Swiss lakes, and defensible fortresses on heights overlooking agricultural land; these were occupied for longer periods than the villages just mentioned. We know, however, very little of habitations in Brittany, Britain, or the Baltic area linked with the culture of the great stone monuments or the Early Bronze Age.

Europe was becoming active in the civilized world. Grain was becoming acclimatized and a factor in its life. Europe could then begin to reap the advantages of her climate, much like the present, but warmer in summer. In this climate surplus heat of the body may be dispersed quickly without overmuch risk of undue cooling, provided clothes are worn. The loess lands had acquired population, as had the alluvial muds on the shores of Swiss lakes, as well as those in the basin of the Po. There was much scope for the expansion of settlements and movement of population.

The chief data concerning the race types of that time are from graves, many of which were discussed in *The Way of the Sea*. Some information is available concerning over 1,000 individuals, but it is often very incomplete, sometimes only the cephalic index being given. A review of skeletons found dating from the end of the Stone Age and the dawn of the Bronze Age is now in progress.

Hunters and Artists, in the appendix to chapter 8, gave a list of some of the best-known skulls and skeletons, dating from the close of the European Palaeolithic Age or the succeeding Epipalaeolithic Age; these came chiefly from Ofnet in Bavaria, Mugem in Portugal, and Furfooz in Belgium, and the list included early British skulls of dubious date. The skulls concerned contrasted with those given at the end of chapter 5 of the same volume from the Upper Palaeolithic Age in Europe. The latter generally show very marked long-headedness; indeed, apart from the finds at Solutré, which are not dated very clearly, there are only two doubtful cases of cranial indices above 76·9; moreover, half the well-authenticated skulls of this period have indices below 73. The skulls from Solutré include some long heads, even extreme long heads, but also a number with indices from 77 to 83. Their distinctness from other upper Palaeolithic finds is, in any case, a marked feature. Continental Epipalaeolithic skulls are strikingly different from the above. Only a few have cranial indices below 73 and only a quite moderate proportion have indices between 73 and 77; well over one-half have indices over 77, but the total numbers are very small. The indices, however, range right up to 88. Britain has yielded a number of narrow skulls dubiously Upper Palaeolithic or Epipalaeolithic.

It may thus be that Epipalaeolithic skulls with cranial indices below 73 represent in Europe an old type, while skulls with indices well over 77 seem to represent a later introduction, or, possibly in some cases, a modification of older types.

In the late Neolithic and the early Bronze Age in western Europe a very long narrow skull is again abundant, but, this time, especially on the loess of Silesia and its continuation in north-west Germany, though it is found almost everywhere. Its relative importance is, however, less than in the Upper Palaeolithic Age. It may be a survival of Upper Palaeolithic types of the loess area, modified, no doubt, or it may be related to a spread along the loess belt of the steppe peoples of south Russia. In any case the very long heads of this age have narrower noses and longer thinner faces than have many of the Palaeolithic long heads. In this connexion we would draw attention to the probability that the Baltic Late Stone Age civilization, especially of the battle-axes, came from the steppe of Russia, as suggested in *The Steppe and the Sown*.

In Britain, again, long skulls, including extreme cases, are so characteristic of 'long barrows' and quasi-contemporary graves that we have the dictum 'Long barrow, long skull'.

In Denmark, especially in the single graves, broad heads are fairly numerous. Whereas in Sweden only about 8 skulls out of about 66 known have indices above 80, 38 have indices below 76; in Denmark, on the other hand, 46 have indices over 80 and only 41 below 76, out of a total of 142 described. A broadheaded element had thus by this time become important in Denmark; it seems to have come in by land rather than by sea. German finds resemble Swedish rather than Danish, but the Beaker Folk stand apart, and to them some Danish skulls are related.

FIG. 2. Central European broad heads.
a, b—A Czech.   *c*—A German (Martin Luther)   *d, e*—Dinaric types.

Data from Switzerland are not abundant, but show a considerable proportion of broad heads, though not many of the Beaker type. In the department of Morbihan in Brittany long skulls are predominant at this period; they are also important in the megalithic area of the Cevennes in south France, though some broad skulls have been found both in south France and in Finistère, Brittany. On the other hand, towards the Ardennes and in the east of the Paris basin, many broad heads have been found. Hervé spoke of an invasion of broad-headed types from the east, along the hills. We may contrast with this the fact that skulls of this period from the Iberian peninsula not only are long-headed but recall those of the Upper Palaeolithic Age; only a few are broad-headed. Skulls of this date from Italy are not numerous, but about as many have indices over 80 as have indices below 76; of the latter most have indices below 74.

Broad-headed elements had thus by this time come to be a conspicuous feature in east and north-east France, and, we may add, northern France, and were also of importance in Switzerland, south-east France, and north Italy. A special variety of broad head, namely, the Beaker type, was present in Germany and was related to a considerable broad-headed element in Denmark. The Beaker type, with finely arched skull, prominent brow ridges, and strong but often short and rounded face, is characteristic of many 'round barrows' in Britain, and persists in modern populations in Britain and central Europe.

Some Round Barrow and Short Cist interments of Aberdeenshire reveal a type more akin to the ordinary broad head mentioned at the beginning of the previous paragraph. We seem to be in face of a spread of Epipalaeolithic (e.g. Ofnet) broad heads. Reche suggests a Mongolian origin via South Russia. Myres, however, probably more wisely, thinks the type spread from the Anatolian-Armenian region, where further evolution has occurred, resulting in the Eastern Alpine or

Tauric-Dinaric type with broad high head, very prominent nose, and rather tall stature. This specialized type is found in the Dinaric Alps and Asia Minor, while the more ordinary round head occurs both in the Alps and their borders towards the west, and in the Hindu Kush and the Pamirs to the east. It may thus be an early type, pushed out in both directions from its original centre of evolution, in both cases among the highlands, the plains being already occupied by long-headed populations. The type in Europe is usually called the Alpine type, though this is open to objection. The Beaker type may be a cross between it and older long-headed types; the Dinaric type is probably an intensified development of the original stock.

Apart from Beaker interments and from Denmark, the Alpine type rarely occurs alone in any numbers in early graves; it often has long-headed types associated with it. The Beaker type occurs most characteristically alone, though a few long skulls do occur with Beaker interments.

In southern and, to some extent, western France, Britain and Sweden, the skulls of the end of the Stone Age are mostly long-headed, with head height moderate in proportion to head length, but nearly equal to, or more than, head breadth. The face is generally narrow and long, and thus more like that of the Predmost-Combe Capelle type than that of the Cromagnon, described in chapter 5 of *Hunters and Artists*; the nose is, however, usually narrow. The type is found most commonly in megalithic graves, and the question must be left open for the present as to whether it is a local evolution from Palaeolithic ancestry, with special narrowing of the nose, or an immigrant type. It could be matched among ancient skulls from the eastern Mediterranean, and is akin to that of contemporary narrow skulls in Central Europe.

Long heads from south-west Europe seem often rather low-headed in Spain and Portugal, but less so in Italy and

Switzerland. Skulls from Spanish megalithic monuments, to judge from drawings, make one hesitate about grouping them very closely with those of France, Britain, and the Baltic; but this needs more investigation. Spanish types, with relatively broad noses, suggest the modern Mediterranean race, while those farther north, with narrow noses, are more akin to the Nordic. The broad-headed types of Central Europe have already been interpreted as forerunners of the Alpine race. On the whole, therefore, already in the Early Bronze Age, the areas of the future Nordic, Alpine, and Mediterranean races of Europe, and of their variants, were fairly marked out, though we cannot as yet say in what measure Nordic and Mediterranean groups were immigrants at the end of the Stone Age, or in what measure they are descendants of western Europeans of the Old Stone Age. Probably both origins are valid for portions of this population. In the Basque provinces of Spain, in the Dordogne in France, in Germany and in Dalarne in Sweden there apparently survive people who, with long heads and short faces and rather tall stature, carry what is supposed by some to be the type of the 'Old Man' of Cromagnon, but this is disputed in the cases of Germany and Sweden.

The so-called Alpine type is not often found in Early Iron Age graves; often those of military leaders in a period of movement and local poverty, due to a wet, cold phase of climate. It is, however, probable that the Alpine race in the modern population of central Europe descends from the broad-headed types discussed above, and it is traditionally interested in peasant agriculture and handicrafts, a fact worth setting beside Myres' view that the type came to Europe from south-west Asia, a region which, as this series has endeavoured to show, was one of the earliest homes of grain cultivation and the crafts. In historic times the broad-headed Alpine element has obviously spread as a peasantry, sometimes apparently swamping older

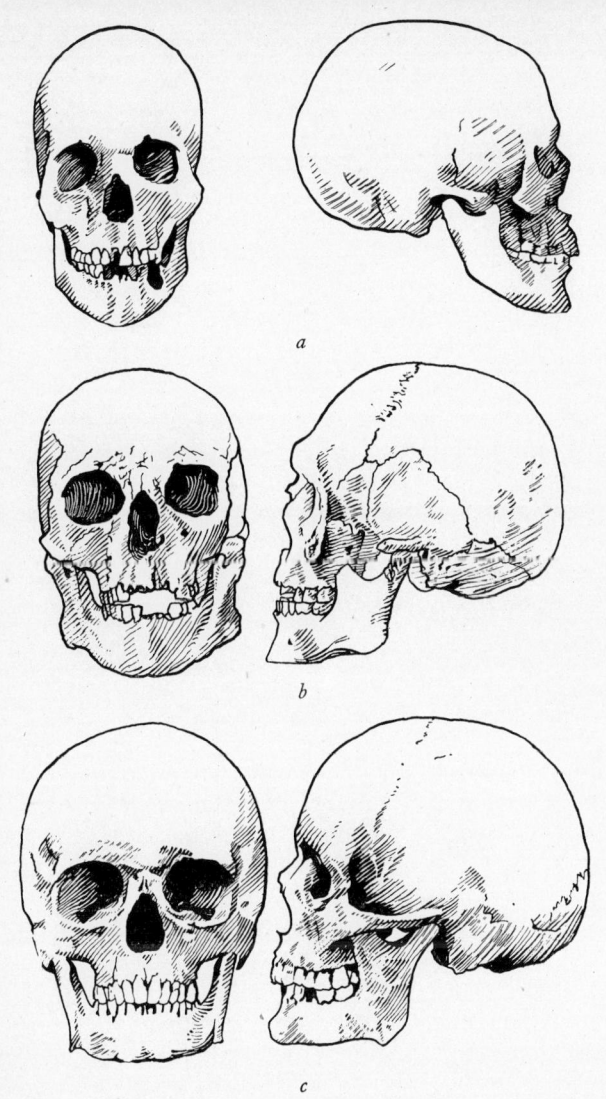

FIG. 3. *a.* Skull from Rotschloss (Aunjetitz Culture). *b.* Skull from Ilderton, Northumberland. *c.* Central European broad head.

long-headed stocks. One of its great spreads has been eastwards from the Galician loess of Poland, past Kiev into the forests of central Russia. There it has met broad-headed and sometimes flat-faced elements coming in from Asia along the steppes of south Russia, or nearer the forest borders farther north.

Among other large features of the distribution of race types, subsequent to the time under discussion in this chapter, may be mentioned the spread of Nordic types southwards, especially in pre-Roman and post-Roman times, while allusion has been made in *The Way of the Sea* to the nests of stalwart dark broad heads in coastal positions around the south-west and west of Europe. Of the period of this spread of dark broad heads we prefer to say little at present, but we think it may be the Bronze Age. We have thus to some extent an outline picture of the evolution of racial distributions in Europe.

Probably Aryan speech had not yet reached Mediterranean lands in the Early Bronze Age, though it may have come as near as the Anatolian plateau. The late Sir John Morris Jones noticed supposed ancient features, which he thought are embedded in the Welsh language and are related to north African tongues. Wales has been so essentially a refuge of ancient cultures, and has been so repeatedly touched on its various fringes, of both land and sea, by newer cultures from time to time, that such a survival is not impossible.

It is difficult to date the Indo-Aryan conquest of India much after the middle of the second millenium B.C.; this conquest brought Aryan speech from the steppes of western Asia to India. The Aryan language family would seem, therefore, to have been established on the steppe well before 1500 B.C., and it seems reasonable to suppose that it was in one form or another the speech of Russian steppe-peoples.

Villages and fortified refuges were in Europe north of the Alps the usual types of settlement, the latter generally on some height. That the temporary settlement gave place to the permanent village seems indicated by the persistence of habitation on many patches of loess. A permanent village probably means some rotation of crops, but we lack evidence of the early plough

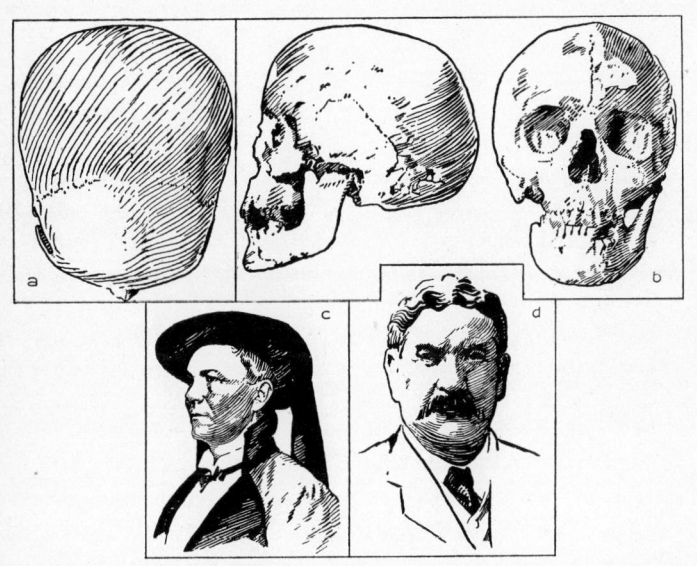

FIG. 4. Broad-headed types from coastal regions. *a*. Skull from Anghelu Ruju, Sardinia; *b*. Skull from El Argar; *c*. A Breton dark broad head (M. le Rouzic); *d*. A Welsh dark broad head (Sir Vincent Evans).

if, indeed, anything but the hoe was used at this time in Europe. Meitzen thought scattered communities, with houses separate from one another, each on its compact farm land, characterized Atlantic Europe until post-Roman times, but in Brittany and the Channel Islands, long considered regions of scattered communities, this form has succeeded a village system. It is thus now doubtful whether the system of scattered homes is primitive anywhere in Europe, but all direct evidence belongs to periods long after the Bronze Age.

Neither in the first evolution of European intercourse, nor in the subsequent development of Europe in the Early Bronze Age, did the idea of the city spread beyond the Aegean region. The nearest approach seems to have been the settlement at El Argar in south-east Spain. Too high a development of intercourse is apparently necessary as a factor of the rise of cities for this feature to be possible in the dawn of the Metal Age in western Europe. This absence of cities would be all the more understandable if we could think of the people, who moved coastwise along the west, as composed largely of seekers for metal, exploiting one source after another. Whether this be legitimate or not as an interpretation, it seems certain that the coastwise communications of the west had stations, in which men were interested in exchanging products and observing ritual. This combination of interests is highly characteristic of many areas, notably the deserts of central Asia, Arabia, and the Sahara of modern times; and in those regions some of the chief stations have developed into cities, such as Mecca, Medina, Riadh, Samarkand, and Bokhara. There is little doubt that a market easily grows at a place of spiritual prestige, which usually becomes a resort of pilgrims.

BOOKS

RIPLEY, W. Z. *The Races of Europe* (London, 1899).
HADDON, A. C. *Races of Man* (Cambridge, 1924).
FLEURE, H. J. *The Peoples of Europe* (Oxford, 1922).

2
The Early Bronze Age in Western Europe

THE terms Neolithic and Bronze Age, and still more that of the Copper Age, must be used with reserve. Copper and gold were the first metals used in far-off times in Mesopotamia and Egypt; this knowledge spread more slowly than the art of grinding stone, which needed less organization. Moreover, copper was relatively soft unless something were mixed with it, accidentally or intentionally, to harden it, and experience taught men that the best substance to add to copper for this purpose was tin. Much experiment was needed before the best mixture was discovered. More than this, the art could be practised only by those who held the secret, and who also had the organization to obtain supplies of both copper and tin. A combination of metallurgists and merchants was essential, and we cannot but suspect that this combination was early effected in the city of Hissarlik II. *The Way of the Sea* noted traces of connexions of Hissarlik II, both by means of the Isthmus of Corinth and Sicily to Spain, and along the Danube valley to Bohemia. As both the Iberian peninsula and Bohemia are known to have been sources of tin, these connexions at least suggest a possibility. Both were early European centres of bronze work, and examples of bronze implements characteristic of the later days of Hissarlik II have been found in both, so it is probable that Hissarlik had much to do with the spread of bronze culture to Europe. This need not be held to imply a belief that Hissarlik was the place where bronze was first invented; Desch has recently analysed fragments of a metal bowl from the grave of Queen Shubad at Ur of the Chaldees and finds that it contained 8·5 per cent. of tin; this may be an important clue to the problem of the origin of bronze.

Agents from Hissarlik II may have sought tin, and copper too, in many lands without spreading the secret. Outlying areas might well have remained for long without metal, save perhaps an occasional implement left by a merchant, though they were in contact with a bronze-using civilization. In the early days of bronze, also, when this alloy was scarce, implements would be well cared for, and, when worn down, bent and blunted, would be remelted rather than cast aside. A district may, therefore, have had bronze implements for some time before the first one was dropped or left for archaeologists to find. The contrast in this relation between bronze and pottery is very striking.

Another factor has undoubtedly added to our difficulties. Burial from very early times has been associated with ritual, and ritual, as consecrated custom, is essentially conservative, so we can understand that the introduction of metal into tombs might well be delayed long after metal was known in the neighbourhood. When we reflect that, on the one hand, a metal implement could be remelted and converted into a new one, and on the other there were men skilled in making the older tools of stone, we understand that a number of human motives worked together to delay the first placing of bronze in tombs. And it is especially tombs that yield evidence of early cultures in western Europe.

Hissarlik II was destroyed about 1900 B.C., and about this time the art of bronze-casting spread to regions with which that city had had connexions. This does not date the first introduction of bronze, much less of metal, into central and western Europe. We are thinking rather of cultures that had bronze-smelting as an activity and, in this chapter, of bronze cultures in west and south-west Europe.

In the Iberian peninsula several stations of this period in the provinces of Almeria in the south-east and of Granada in the south were examined by Siret, who found some 1,300 interments. The chief station is that of El Argar in Almeria. Here burial without burning was the invariable rule, and sometimes a cist was made; at other times a few stones were placed around the body. In the vast majority of the cases, however, the remains were placed in an urn. The largest number of skeletons in one burial was three, so there is no question here of communal burial. In the tombs are great urns, containing the corpse and provisions, and along with these occur cylindrical pots with a somewhat hollowed base, as well as biconical vessels, both of which recall pottery of the megalithic culture. There are, however, also bowls on high footstands, which are distinctive Contrasting still more markedly with the furniture of megalithic tombs is the wealth of metal objects and the poverty in those of stone, but there is not the marked evolution of metallurgy that one finds farther north.

Among the most typical copper objects are axes, which may be hammered flat and have the cutting edge expanded, but have often been cast. The flat axe, of copper or bronze, is primarily a Mediterranean feature, associated with the cultures of the eastern Mediterranean generally, and thus, naturally, also with those of the coasts of the Iberian peninsula, and especially with El Argar. With the flat metal axe, essentially a modified metal copy of a polished stone axe, there appears the short dagger. One finds stone axes that copy metallic forms, as well as metal axes adjusted from types known in stone. The dagger, however, showed other possibilities. It seems to begin as a small triangular plate of copper, moulded, and then, in some cases, hammered to give a point. Rivet-holes bored through the base are a typical addition; they may be set in a straight or curved line across the base, and tell us that the dagger was mounted on the end of a holder, probably of wood. The riveting also indicates that the early metallurgists did not use soldering. The dagger was liable to bend, especially because of the power gained through having a holder. This danger was lessened by giving the blade a median rib or thickening. A tang was another early feature, supplementing the rivets; this feature, at home at Hissarlik, is relatively rare in the west. Another possibility offered itself. The holder could be fixed at right-angles to the main axis of the blade, and thus there evolved the halberd, known to French archaeologists as the *hache-poignard*. As the weapon had a short haft and was used as an axe, the term knife-axe would be more appropriate. The metal blade of the halberd or knife-axe is usually strengthened by a median rib. About a dozen halberds have been found at El Argar, but daggers are far more numerous. There are a few swords, but these on general grounds would be supposed to belong to a later phase of the culture, though one could not argue this from El Argar.

Copper arrow-heads, more or less like those of stone, mark very particularly the contrast between this culture and those discussed in *The Way of the Sea*. Rings, bracelets, and diadems in copper, bronze, and silver, and some few in gold, are other features, as are beads of the most varied materials, including callais, a subject discussed in *The Way of the Sea*. Some of the bone beads are segmented and early, and a few segmented beads in glass, found with a bronze sword, have been gathered from a later interment. Provisionally, we consider the culture of El Argar the successor of, and substitute for, the culture of Los Millares, found in a number of settlements in which stone was largely used. Though Mediterranean France is poor in bronze hoards, in the forelands of the south French Alps there are rock carvings, including representations of daggers hafted to a holder at right-angles to the main axis; these carvings will be discussed in chapter 4.

The Early Metal Age in the Iberian peninsula was an extension of that age in the Aegean and the eastern Mediterranean generally. Much of the cultural development discussed in *The Way of the Sea* was earlier than that now described, but there

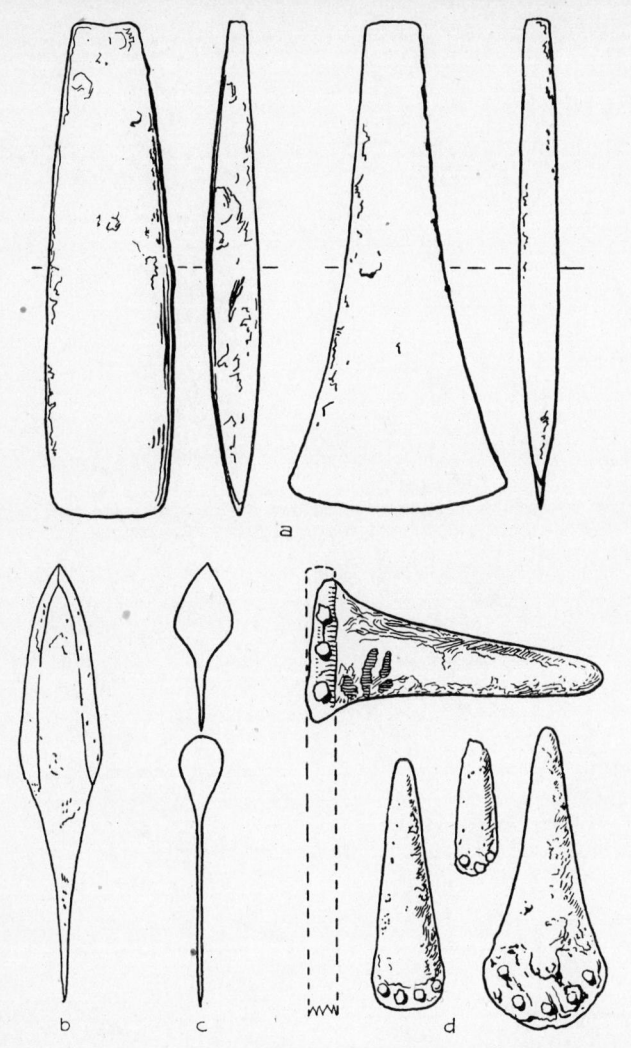

FIG. 5. *a.* Early metal axes; *b.* Tanged point, copper, Aljezor, S. Portugal; *c.* Tanged points, copper, Palmella; *d.* Early halberd-blade and daggers, El Oficio, Almeria, Spain.

were probably many overlaps, and there is no small likelihood that much of that early culture, worked out in stone, owed a good deal to metal cultures already existing in the eastern Mediterranean. The art of metallurgy may have been transplanted from the eastern Mediterranean, perhaps at a late stage of the history of Hissarlik II, perhaps when that city fell. The peoples of the eastern Mediterranean seem to have been interested in Iberian metallic ores.

The early metal culture of the Iberian peninsula is weak; it does not expand into a rich and characteristically local culture as does that which began rather later in the west Baltic region. Metallurgy is an activity which exhausts one source of supply after another, and one might pick hundreds of examples, from Ireland to Australia, of derelict mineral workings of various periods. Probably the early metallurgists of Europe looked to stream-sands for both tin and gold, and did not crush the ores concerned. Exhaustion of supplies would come about sooner or later, and metallurgists would move on. If the Iberian cultures, discussed in *The Way of the Sea*, were related to those of the early days of metallurgy in the eastern Mediterranean, the supplies of metalliferous river-sand in the Iberian peninsula may well have been exhausted fairly early, the metallurgists moving onwards to newer supplies farther away. The cultures thus transported step by step would have had little object in maintaining the link with the eastern Mediterranean through the Iberian peninsula when the sands there had become exhausted. The fall of Hissarlik II, the rise of Knossos, and, in all probability, the growing exhaustion of Iberian supplies of metal, would all tend to cut off the West from the East, and the West, apparently, went on its independent way.

Up to some years ago thirteen hoards of metal had been found in France containing no axes beyond the simple flat type, ten in departments on or near the Atlantic seaboard, reaching as far north as Brittany, and one each in the departments of Aisne, Indre, and Isère. Only one hoard of this class occurs near the English Channel, east of Brittany, an important feature, because these departments, especially the lower Seine, are rich in Middle Bronze Age hoards, while Manche has over 100 of the Late Bronze Age. The distribution of hoards, containing metal axes of both flat and flanged types, but none more advanced, is also characteristic. Along the Atlantic seaboard, as far north as Brittany, there are twenty-three such hoards, seventeen of which were found in the department of Gironde, but eight hoards occur in departments adjoining the above, including six in the departments of the Norman coast west of the Seine. There are in this case seven hoards in departments of the centre and the Alpine east, and seven in the south away from the Atlantic. The Atlantic coast thus yields far more hoards of the Early Bronze Age than other parts of the country (see Fig. 33). The same point was made in the discussion of megalithic monuments, and here again, as in the case of the Iberian peninsula, we cannot be sure that we are dealing with totally distinct periods. The megalithic monuments are primarily tombs and give us tomb furniture—that is, ritual objects; the bronze hoards are more related to commercial life. Le Rouzic recently found in dolmen No. 2 at Parc-er-Guren, Morbihan, a segmented bead of green-blue faience with a fragment of a triangular dagger of copper, an indication of the continuation of interest in megalithic tombs after metal had been introduced. Such evidence is, however, hardly needed, as these monuments are associated still, in folk tradition, with ancient rites and ceremonies, often very clearly of pre-Christian origin.

The discovery of segmented bone tubes with an early triangular dagger in the dolmen of Cabut, Gironde, is further important evidence of Iberian connexions.

The sands of the Vilaine in Brittany yield tin, and what are now islands off the Breton coast, Houat, Hoedic, and Belle Île, have yielded tin and gold, and this so impressed Siret that he concluded they were the Cassiterides of tradition. France was not a unit in Early Bronze Age times, and the country, apart from the Atlantic seaboard, was probably of small importance. The Alpine east, with its bronze axes that have raised edges or flanges fairly like those of the Atlantic coast, was probably an

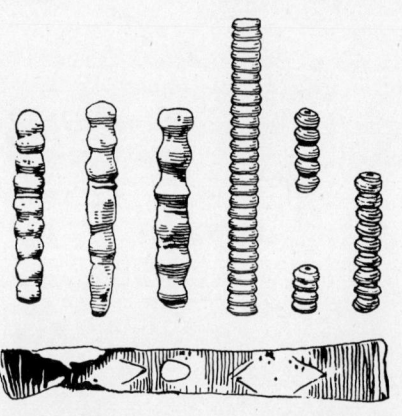

FIG. 6. Segmented beads and bone tubes.

extension of a central European province of culture, or a link between such a province and that of the Atlantic seaboard, as will be argued in chapter 5.

England yields scattered flat axes of bronze or copper and a fair number of simple triangular daggers in the Downlands of Dorset and Wiltshire, as well as in east Yorkshire; others occur scattered over the country. They extend into north Wales, but are relatively scarce in the west of Britain. There are hints of the beginnings of routes from the Downs of south England across to the Mersey, on which there may have been a port at or near Warrington, and to north-west Wales, in which area the region

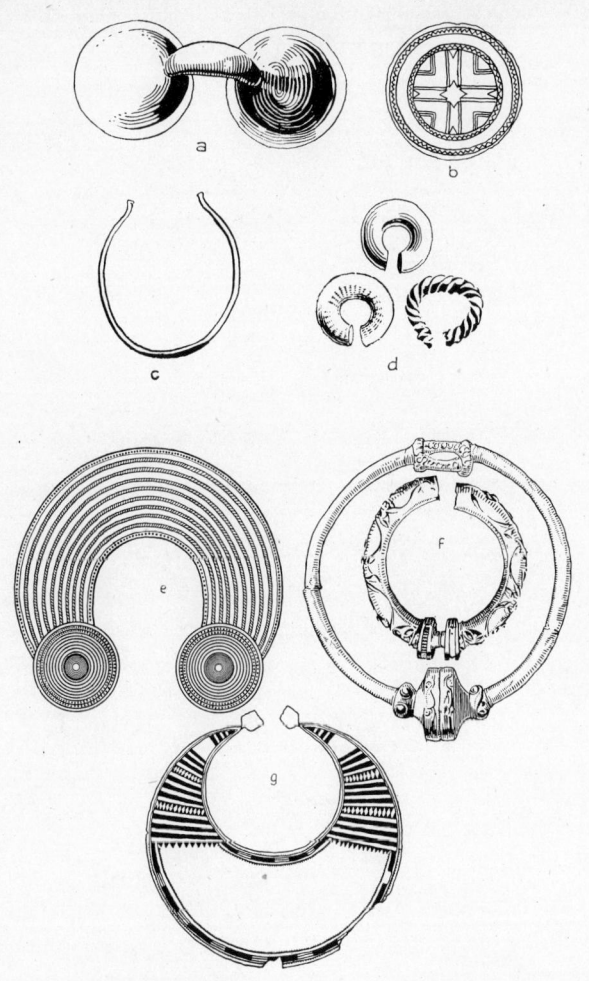

FIG. 7. Gold ornaments from Ireland. *a*. 'Fasteners'; *b*. Sun disk; *c*. Thin pennanular ring; *d*. Pennanular rings; *e*. Gorget; *f*. Torcs; *g*. Crescent or lunula.

These objects probably date from various phases of the Bronze Age.

that stretches around the north-east shore of Cardigan Bay, played an important part in the Bronze Age as in early historic times. Britain has some flanged bronze axes, but much fewer than France.

The earliest types of implements found in Ireland include flat copper axes and a few simple daggers and halberds. Some Irish ornaments of gold may belong to the very beginning of the Bronze Age, but Coffey hesitated to suggest so early a date, though at Harlyn Bay near Padstow in Cornwall an early Irish gold ornament has been found in association with a flat axe. The Irish dagger and flat axe, especially of copper, are related to those of Atlantic France and the Iberian peninsula, a hint of a continuation, and it may be an expansion, of the maritime connexion discussed in *The Way of the Sea*. Ireland is rich in copper but has no tin; there is thus considerable reason for thinking that the Copper Age may have lasted for a long time in Ireland. Cornwall had both copper and tin, while Alderley Edge and many other places produced copper; Britain would, therefore, not be forced to look to Ireland for supplies of copper. A careful study of Irish halberds led Much to the view that they are later than those of the Iberian peninsula, which may have served them as models, but earlier than those of central Europe.

The coming of metallurgy apparently makes no break in the schemes of cultural intercourse in the Iberian peninsula, France, or the British Isles, but it leads to local developments in the two latter. Elements, which may be of central European origin, naturally play a greater part in France than in Britain, and in both these countries than in Ireland.

Rich alluvial gold in the Wicklow Hills was extensively worked, and gold objects of undoubted Irish workmanship have been found in many parts of the continent. The gold of Wicklow was worked even late in the eighteenth century of our era. It is worth noting in this connexion that Glendalough, in the heart of the Wicklow Hills, was one of the sacred centres of early Christianity in Ireland. Curiously enough, St. David's in south Wales and Santiago da Compostella in Spanish Galicia were also important early Christian centres, and seem to have been of

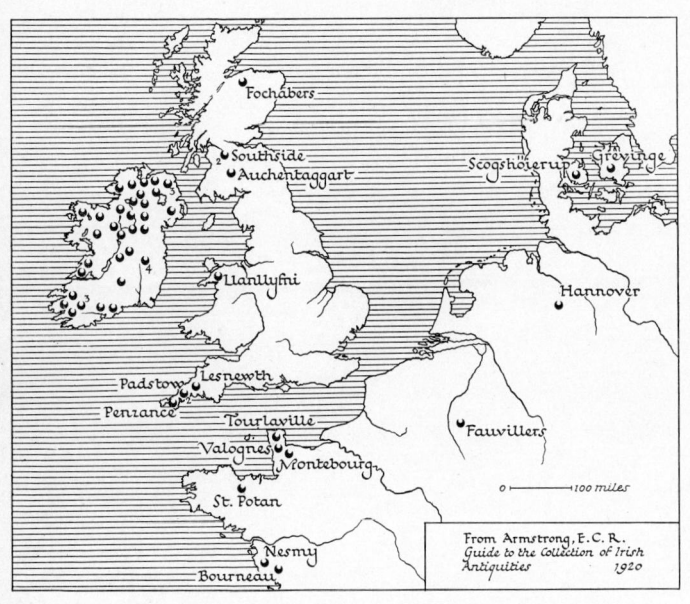

FIG. 8. Map showing the distribution of gold crescents. By permission of the Controller, Stationery Office, Dublin.

consequence in prehistoric times as well. This suggests that Glendalough was also of importance in these early times.

The best-known Bronze Age gold objects from Ireland are the crescents or *lunulae*, found plentifully in that island as well as occasionally in other places. They are fine crescent-shaped plates of gold, covered with indented geometric ornament at each end of the crescent and often along the edges as well. Outside

Ireland, one has been found at Llanllyfni in Carnarvonshire, one at Penzance, another at Lesnewth, and two at Harlyn Bay in Cornwall, one in Dumfriesshire, another in Morayshire, and two in Lanarkshire, six in France, including one in Côtes-du-Nord, two in Vendée, and three in Manche, one, of a slightly different type, so M. l'Abbé Breuil has told one of us, in north-west Spain, one at Fauvillers in Luxembourg, one near Hannover, and two in Denmark—in Fünen and Zealand respectively. None have datable associations except those from Harlyn Bay near Padstow, which were found with a flat axe of bronze. This, if the axe was not a very belated specimen when buried, indicates that the gold trade of Ireland grew in the Early Bronze Age. The route from Ireland to Denmark perhaps crossed Scotland, or passed across England, Holland, and part of Germany, while the discoveries at Harlyn Bay and Penzance indicate both ends of a transpeninsular route across Cornwall—a route also used, apparently, in the Middle Ages. This route seems to have crossed the English Channel to the neighbourhood of Cherbourg, and to have passed down Manche and through Vendée on its way to north-west Spain. Necklaces of jet, resembling these crescents in shape, have been found in some numbers in Scotland.

The National Museum, Dublin, has twenty-four gold torcs; similar objects have been found in England and France, while one, closely resembling these, was discovered at Hissarlik II. As none have been found either in the west Baltic region or in the Iberian peninsula, that found at Hissarlik can only with great difficulty be considered as related to those of the west, especially since a torc of this type was found at Grunty Fen, Cambridgeshire, apparently in association with three looped palstaves of a not very early type; it must be admitted, however, that the palstaves were found twelve inches above the torc. Nevertheless we must not forget the similarly isolated discovery of callais beads, objects typical of Portugal, Spain, southern France, and

Brittany at the dawn of the Metal Age, at Kadi Keui on the shores of the Sea of Marmora at no great distance from the site of Hissarlik. Recent growth of knowledge concerning intercourse over long distances during the Early Bronze Age makes such thoughts less improbable than formerly.

The pottery of the Early Bronze Age has as yet been insufficiently studied in France. Four-handled jars are a characteristic

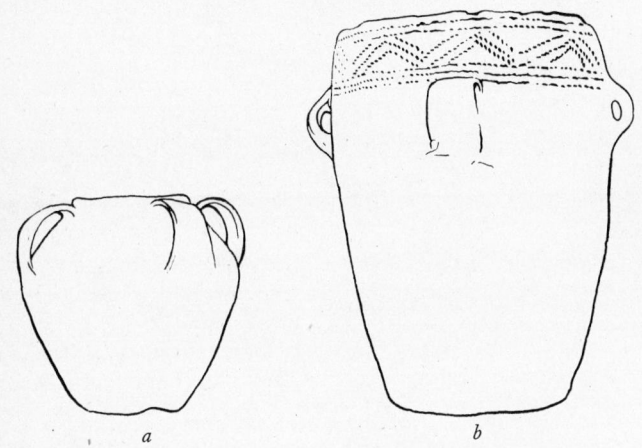

FIG. 9. Four-handled jars from (*a*) Finistère, (*b*) Cornwall.

type in Brittany, and some have been found in Cornwall. They may be urn-shaped or more or less biconical, and allied forms have been unearthed in the south of France, Sicily, Bohemia, and the Rhineland, but are nowhere so characteristic as in Brittany. Deeply incised ornament often occurs on Early Bronze Age pottery in France; it may take the form of bands, or of triangular areas of parallel grooves. The British Bronze Age pottery differs from that of the beaker and megalithic cultures in being local and Irish, with cinerary urns, food vessels, some beakers of local type which lingered on, and small vessels that have been called incense cups, and often show a pair of holes through the side. The pottery is not of such fine paste and workmanship as the best beakers, and it seems as though indigenous feeling were penetrating the craft at the expense of the immigrant stimulus brought in by the makers of the beakers; in practically all cases it is funereal pottery.

In our islands, at the far end of the ancient world, beaker and megalithic cultures lingered on and contributed to what in

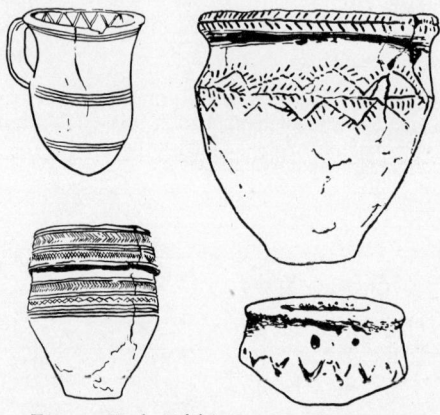

FIG. 10. Early British Bronze Age pottery.

later times, after the advent of Celtic speech, came to be known as the civilization of the Celtic fringe. In Ireland the chief kind of Bronze Age pottery is the food vessel, developed from the round-bottomed bowl of Iberian origin, described in *The Way of the Sea*, and spreading from Ireland chiefly across the north of England. M. l'Abbé Breuil has kindly informed us of a close correspondence of design between the conventionalized staghorn design on an Irish urn and the ornament on pottery from the Pileta Cave in Malaga, and a site in the Sierra Nevada, Sa. del Castillo, Almaden, in the province of Ciudad Real, Spain.

FIG. 11. The spiral at New Grange.

The continuance of megalithic culture is illustrated by the famous alignments of Carnac, which pass over an interment that is apparently of the Early Bronze Age; they are not likely, therefore, to be older than that period. In Ireland the famous corbelled tombs, the chief example of which is New Grange, are often ascribed to the Early Bronze Age. The spiral decoration seen on the door-stone of New Grange originated at one or more places in the eastern Mediterranean, and the idea may have reached Ireland by means of the west Baltic, since the stone cultures of those two regions are largely akin, or from south-west Europe, as seems to us more probable in view of the widespread habit of engraving on the surface of megalithic monuments, and of the use of the spiral, or of forms akin to it, in Malta, Sicily, and Brittany. A spiral engraved on a great stone occurs in Wales, at Llanbedr in Merionethshire, and something akin to this on the remarkable monument at Bryn Celli Du in Anglesey.

The stone circles of Britain, as well as the alignments of Brittany, date, we believe, from the Early or Middle Bronze Age in what was later to become the Celtic fringe, and to them a short chapter is devoted. Another peculiarity is the cremation of the dead in Brittany, as against burial, the usual practice in Europe at that time.

The early bronze culture of the west Baltic region may be another aspect of the culture of the megalithic tombs and single graves discussed in *The Way of the Sea*, or, at least, of its later phases. The earliest bronze objects found in graves include swords and axes of highly specialized types. The Early Bronze Age has, however, left us flat axes, mostly of copper; they occur sporadically and not in graves, and the thought forces itself upon one that, when these objects were in use, the stone culture was still persisting and stone objects were still being placed in the graves. Maps by Lissauer and Åberg showing the distributions of both stone cultures and early copper and bronze implements suggest on the whole a link between Denmark and central Europe; that link became greatly reinforced when the amber exchange developed between the Danish shores and Bohemia.

The introduction of metals into the west of Europe was thus, in our opinion, attended by no immediate revolution; the cultures described in *The Way of the Sea* continued to express social experience, but tended towards local developments, specially characteristic in the west Baltic, owing to the amber traffic, and in Ireland in consequence of the trade in gold. The Iberian peninsula declined, with some renaissance later on; in France a mingling of Atlantic and central European elements of culture continued into succeeding phases of the Bronze Age, while in Britain, apart from the Downs of the south, the tendency was towards localism, with some loss of cultural initiative. In south Britain the tin supplies of the west played a part in maintaining cultural levels.

BOOKS

CHILDE, V. GORDON. *The Dawn of European Civilization* (London, 1925).
CHILDE, V. GORDON. *The Bronze Age* (Cambridge, 1930).
ABERCROMBY, J. *Bronze Age Pottery* (Oxford, 1912).
COFFEY, G. *New Grange* (Dublin, 1912).
COFFEY, G. *The Bronze Age in Ireland* (Dublin, 1913).
Fox, C. *Archaeology of the Cambridge Region* (Cambridge, 1923).
Archaeologia, Vol. 80, 1930. HEMP, W. J., 'The Chambered Cairn of Bryn Celli Du.'

3
Carnac and Stonehenge

THE fact has already been noted that Britain and Brittany are regions where old-fashioned things have tended to survive.

Carnac in Brittany possesses a unique monument in the great alignments, of which nearly 4 kilometres still remain. The first series, that of Ménec, has eleven lines of standing stones, occupying a zone 100 metres wide and over 1,100 metres in length, with 1,099 stones, varying in height from 60 centimetres to 4 metres. Outlying stones suggest that the lines were once even more numerous. At their western end, pointing about 20° south of west, are 70 standing stones arranged in a semicircle or, as it is called in Brittany, a cromlech. In the British Isles cromlech is a term rather loosely used for many old stone monuments.

To the east of this series, and separated from it by a gap of about 340 metres, are the lines of Kermario, 1,120 metres in length and about the same width as before, though here the number of lines is ten. This series contains 982 standing stones, but no cromlech or semicircle remains at the west end; the general direction is 57° east of north. There are many indications, from outlying stones and from the monuments of Manio discussed below, that here a newer scheme has replaced an older one.

East again, and separated from the Kermario lines by a gap of nearly 400 metres, are the lines of Kerlescant, containing 540 standing stones in thirteen lines, covering a width of nearly 140 metres and a length of 880 metres, and ending in a squarish ring of stones or cromlech, in which 39 stones remain in place.

There are remains of other alignments to the west, and those near Erdeven include a further 1,129 stones. It has been suggested that the alignments once marked off districts from the Étel estuary to that of Ste Barbe and thence to that of Crac'h. Traces of other alignments have been suspected in the district just outside the surviving lines. The whole area is uniquely rich in megalithic monuments, and *The Way of the Sea* described it as, at the period then described, a meeting-place of the cultures of the south-west and north-west.

The Kermario series sets its course right across an area of monuments known as the *Tertre du Manio*, on which stands a

Fig. 12. The Ménec alignments.

great stone that is 4 metres high, whereas those near it have a height of 1 metre. This great stone marks a sepulchral area 54 metres by 35, but raised only 1 metre above the general level, bounded by walling which is triplicate in one part. Within these limits are numerous small stone constructions, mostly rounded or cist-like, often suggesting decadent megaliths; one yielded Early Bronze Age pottery. If, as seems clear, the alignments of Kermario went right across the sepulchral area without taking other notice of it than to incorporate its great standing stone in their scheme, these alignments date after the beginning of the Bronze Age. As Early Iron Age remains are scarce, the building of the lines can hardly have been as late as that period; so they probably belong to some phase of the Bronze Age after the building of the great tombs and some of the cists. They thus represent a late local specialization of the megalithic culture in one of its metropolitan areas. The uniqueness of the scheme in France is extraordinary, the more because standing stones are very numerous in the department of Finistère. Two long avenues, mostly of smallish stones, are a feature near Merivale Bridge and near Cas Tor on Dartmoor, Devon, and it has been thought they once existed in the neighbourhood of Fishguard, Pembrokeshire. Fergusson gives apparently trustworthy evidence of the former existence of avenues of standing stones at Shap, between the Cumbrian mountains and the Pennines, and thought they were related to some stone circles.

The alignment of Ménec, at Carnac, ends in what has been a semicircle of standing stones. Full circles are rare in Brittany, but these, half submerged, are famous at Er Lannic in Le Morbihan. The stone circle, on the other hand, is the most important type of prehistoric stone monument in Great Britain, while the stone avenue is quite subordinate. A wooden circle once existed at Bleasdale in Lancashire, and recently 'Woodhenge' has been discovered on the Salisbury Downs.

The beaker culture reached westward in south England to the Salisbury Downs, and, both before and after metal came in, that area was an important centre, and, we judge, a meeting-place of the beaker and megalith cultures. There are physical reasons for this. The lines of the South and the North Downs, of the East Anglian Heights with the Chilterns, of the Cotswolds and the Mendip and Blackdown Hills, converge here. These are high lines of porous rock that probably never had a close covering of trees, though there may have been hanger woods on the scarp faces. Unforested belts were lines of communication and settlement in the later Stone Age, and stone axes and similar implements are often found on them. The river Avon, with a good entry from the sea at Hengistbury near Christchurch in Hampshire, where later was a famous station of the Early Iron Age, and the possibility of boating up to Amesbury or above, offered a route of entry from the English Channel alternative to those of the Chalk Downs reached through the Solent and Winchester or by Weymouth Bay or Poole Harbour. Bronze Age objects are often found along navigable rivers, and there are suggestions of Bronze Age settlement on patches of river gravel. The Salisbury Downs were thus a focus of landways, and a centre where met alternative hill and river entries from the sea. Moreover, on the Marlborough Downs towards the north were huge blocks of sarsen stones, fragments of an Eocene formation that once covered large parts of the chalk. This admittedly circumstantial evidence suggests an Early or Middle Bronze Age date for a part at least of the famous monument of Stonehenge, and it is surrounded by many barrows of that period.

Stonehenge is reached by an avenue, flanked by ditches, which was discovered by Crawford. There is an encircling earthwork-ditch, surrounding a circle of post-holes, called by Hawley the Aubrey Holes, and now believed to have held wooden posts; farther in, but still outside the stone circle, are two other circles of holes, which probably never held posts. The Aubrey

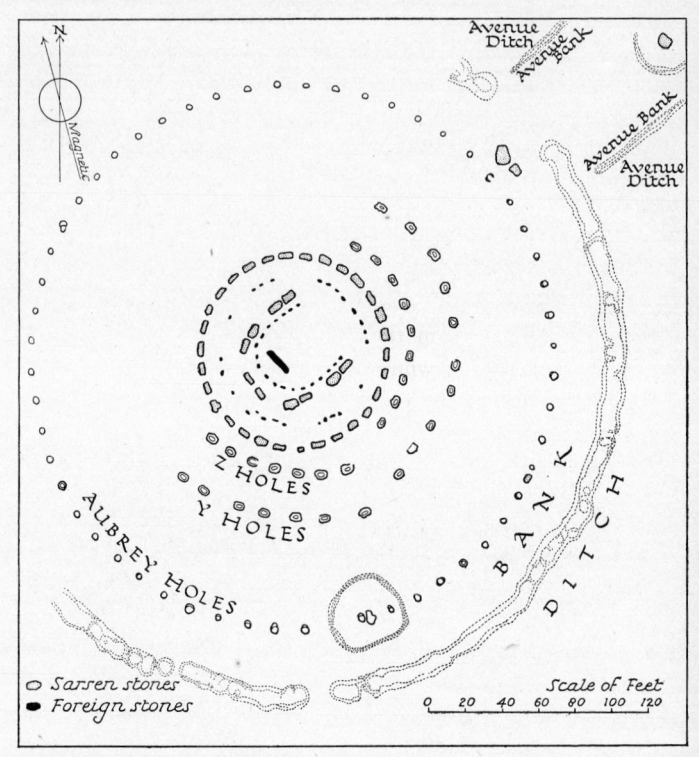

FIG. 13. Plan of Stonehenge. After the plan in *Antiquity*, March 1929, based upon the Survey made by H.M. Office of Works. By permission of the Controller of H.M. Stationery Office.

Holes have mostly yielded traces of burnt human bones, and their filling, for they have been filled up and were revealed by air photography, includes chips of both the local and the foreign stones that make up the four stone circles. The outermost circle of sarsen stones with lintels shows tenon and mortice jointing, a circle next inside it consists of non-local or 'blue' stones, an inner incomplete ring or horseshoe is of sarsen trilithons, and an innermost ring of 'blue' stones. There are also sarsens lying to the north-east and south-west of the circles,

FIG. 14. View of Stonehenge. Royal Air Force official.—Crown copyright reserved.

near the ditch, and, in connexion with the avenue, a great sarsen called the Slaughter Stone and an upright called the Hele or Heel Stone

Thirty-eight foreign stones have been incorporated in the circles at Stonehenge, and H. H. Thomas has found that they are of various types, all occurring in the area between the Preseli Hills and Haverfordwest. They were transported from Pembrokeshire to Stonehenge by those who built or rebuilt the monument, and probably they formed a sacred circle in

Pembrokeshire, a great centre of western megalithic culture, and one of the most important call-points in voyages northward between Brittany and Ireland, a very-much-used route in early times. The feeling gains ground that they were taken to their present site from the river along the avenue mentioned above, and, if so, they probably came from Pembrokeshire by sea, but, if they were transported by land, the feat was all the more remarkable; so in any case we are in the presence of triumphs of prehistoric civil engineering as regards both the building of Stonehenge and the transport of the foreign stones. The megalithic culture was centred especially on western promontories in Britain. The meetings of those megalith and beaker cultures gave rise to considerable local developments from south Spain to the west Baltic. Salisbury Downs were an important focus and a likely centre for such local cultural development.

At Avebury, at the west foot of the Marlborough Downs, are the considerable remains of what was probably the largest stone circle in existence. It has a diameter of about 400 yards and is surrounded by ditch and rampart. Inside the main earth-ring there were two double circles of sarsen stones. There were formerly one, and possibly two, avenues of sarsen stones approaching the monument; one of the nearest of many neighbouring antiquities is the earthwork on Windmill Hill, discussed in *The Way of the Sea*, an important early culture centre. Whether Windmill Hill and Avebury are connected in origin we cannot say, but, near the bottom of the ditch of the latter, was found a fragment of pottery very like some from Windmill Hill.

There are several other stone circles in and near the Chalk country. The largest elsewhere in Britain are as follows: Long Meg and her Daughters near Penrith in north-west England, in Derbyshire Arbor Low is the best known, while that at Callernish, in the Barvas district of Lewis in the Outer Hebrides, and that at Stennis in the Orkneys, are other famous examples.

Carnac and Stonehenge

Another is incorporated in the churchyard wall at Ysbyty Cynfyn in north Cardiganshire; the interest in this case is enhanced by the probability that here is a continuity of sanctity

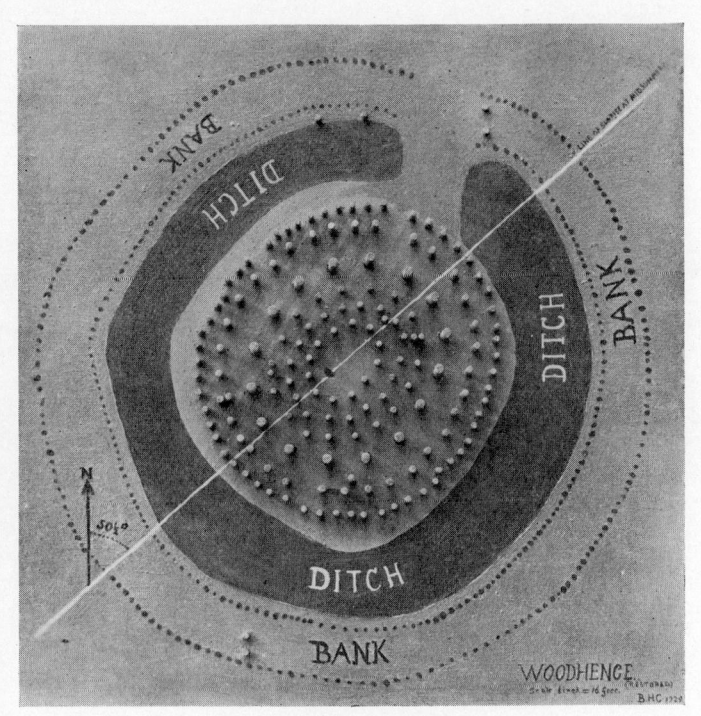

Fig. 15. View of Woodhenge.

from pre-Christian times, and a clue to the roundness of so many churchyards in Wales and elsewhere. St. Germain, near Étel, west of Carnac in Brittany, also has remains of a stone circle partially incorporated in a churchyard wall.

Near Stonehenge traces of six concentric rings of holes have been shown to have held wooden posts, and the discoverers,

Mr. and Mrs. Cunnington, have named this remarkable place 'Woodhenge'. The circle was surrounded by a ditch, and there were other post-holes, not belonging to the ring, to the number of six outside and six inside the ditch. Within the innermost ring was found a child's grave, the skull, apparently, having been cleft before burial. The discoverers have shown that the rings at Woodhenge have a close analogy in measurements with those at Stonehenge, of which they think it a predecessor. The tenon and mortice jointing of pillars and lintels at Stonehenge is a scheme borrowed from woodwork. The Aubrey Holes there probably lodged timber uprights, and similar holes, that also once held posts, have been found (in 1930) by Mrs. Cunnington at The Sanctuary near Avebury. The historical connexion between the monuments still, however, remains uncertain. Pottery contemporary with the latest beakers was still in use when the bank at Woodhenge was thrown up, and fragments show overhanging rims, a feature of early cinerary urns. The discoverers therefore now, with much reserve, date the monument to the Middle Bronze Age or a little earlier.

At Bleasdale, in north Lancashire, have been found the remains of two circles of oaken posts, one within the other, but not concentric, the inner nearly touching the outer on the east. Cinerary urns with overhanging rims were found at the centre of the inner circle. There are other known cases of the use of timber in prehistoric circles, notably at Harendermolen in Holland.

Enough has now been said to suggest that the alignments of Brittany and the stone circles of Great Britain continue the development of megalithic culture well into the Bronze Age. The megalithic culture of Ireland seems to have been more conservative.

Ysbyty Cynfyn suggests continuity of sanctity from the days of stone circles, whatever be their date in west Wales, to Christian times, and in Brittany we have endless indications

FIG. 16. View of Ysbyty Cynfyn.

of the survival of folk ritual gathered around the megaliths, and these practices are more or less incorporated in rites of the Church. A synthesis of megalithic and beaker civilizations seems an important feature in the evolution of the distinctive life of what has become the 'Celtic Fringe', and seems to have retained honour right down to Christian times.

The possibility should be borne in mind that the circle of wooden posts may have been a central European idea, brought westward and expressing itself in stone when it made close contact with the megalithic culture. One needs to remember the diverse distributions of the various evidences of megalithic civilization. The menhir is characteristic of northern France and western Britain. In spite of its great importance in Brittany it is not nearly such a feature of the south-France-to-Brittany zone as is the dolmen.

BOOKS

CUNNINGTON, M. E. *Woodhenge* (Devizes, 1929).
Antiquaries' Journal. Reports on Stonehenge from 1921 onwards.
STEVENS, F. *Stonehenge to-day and yesterday* (London, 1924).

4

The Early Bronze Age in Central Europe

THE Steppe and the Sown, figs. 80–3, illustrated the spread of peasant culture in central Europe soon after the middle of the third millennium B.C. The lands occupied were especially those with a loess subsoil or, as in Switzerland, alluvial areas near lake-shores, and river-valleys, such as the Bavarian Danube, were lines of spread. *The Way of the Sea*, chapter 2, noted relations between these peasant cultures of central Europe and the early bronze-workers of the Aegean and Asia Minor. So long as this intercourse, especially with Hissarlik II, lasted, tin was taken to the Aegean from the Erzgebirge and copper from farther east, from Slovakia or Transylvania; no contemporary bronze object is known from central Europe, though a few of copper occur.

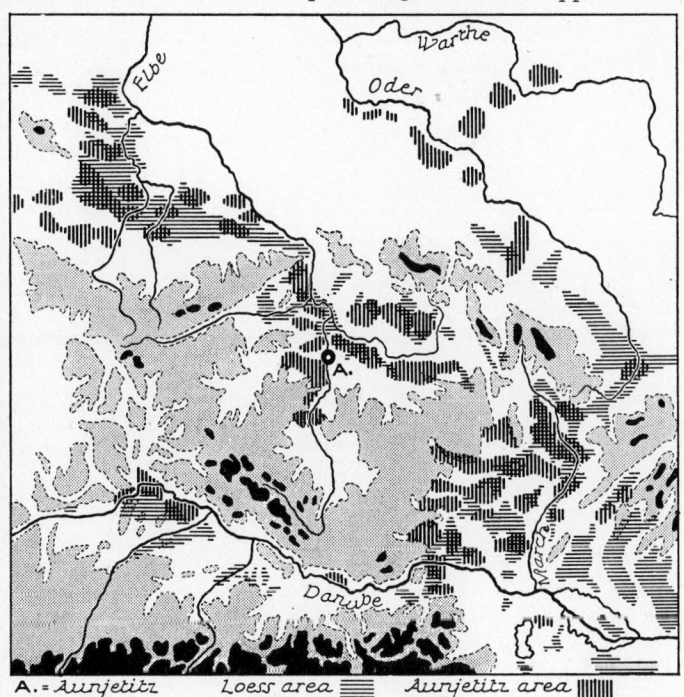

FIG. 17. The Area of the Aunjetitz culture (1,500–3,000 feet = stippled area; over 3,000 feet = black-shaded area).

The fall of Hissarlik II about 1900 B.C. may have disturbed an old system of intercourse, and this event may be linked up with the rather sudden disappearance of the beaker culture.

This culture, in our opinion, belonged to carriers working *inter alia* along the loess of central Europe. Along the foothills of Silesia, on loess and black-earth subsoil, there had developed at this time a variant of the Danubian peasant culture, with contributions from other sources, at Marschwitz. This culture had extended westward *via* the Glatz district and east of the Riesengebirge into north Bohemia and the Erzgebirge. This unexpected route is related to the increase of metallurgy. As the beaker culture declined, and old relations were broken by the fall of Hissarlik, metal working gave birth to the culture of Aunjetitz (Unetiče) in Smichow district near Prague.

Childe has shown that Aegean and Anatolian influences played upon the region of the junctions with the Tisza of rivers rolling down gold-bearing sands from Transylvania, and extended northwards towards the copper-bearing mountains of Slovakia, as well as towards the Hungarian Danube. At the same time stone hammer-axes from Perjamos suggest developments of older South Russian cultural elements that had already spread along the loess through central Europe to the Baltic. Childe derives pottery of the Tisza settlements, Toszeg and Perjamos, from Hissarlik II. Bronze daggers of Cypriote types, torques and pins, tell the same tale even more clearly. Mediterranean shells, *Pectunculus* and *Cardium* species, give further confirmation. Aunjetitz also owed much to older cultures and to infiltration of objects from the Rhine, from the Baltic, and from Spain. It resulted from complex hybridization and development of rich local resources, tin from the Erzgebirge alloyed with copper probably brought in the first instance from Slovakia or Transylvania. *The Way of the Sea* described the rise of long-distance intercourse in Europe; here we touch the rise of industry with importation of material—an important step forward in social complexity.

The copper or bronze dagger of, ultimately, Cretan origin is an Aunjetitz feature, and is thought by some students to have reached central Europe from Spain through the activities of the beaker-people. This is probable.

Central Europe

Bohemia, like other copper-producing areas of the Early Bronze age in Europe, such as the Iberian peninsula, west

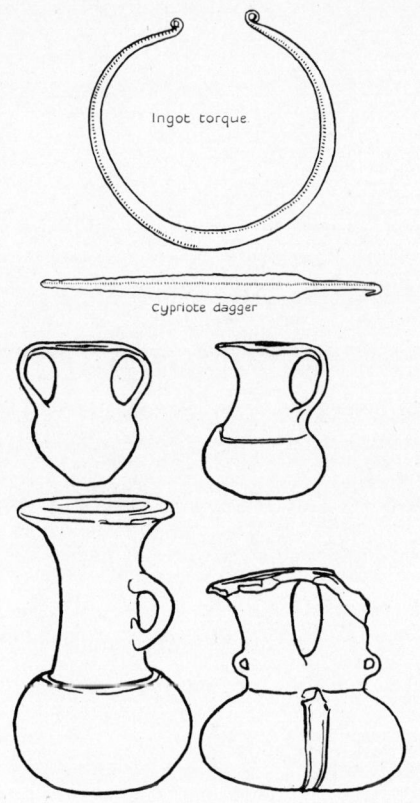

FIG. 18. Objects of Early Metal Age. Hungary. Upper pots Oszentiván, lower pots Tószegh; metal objects Csorvás.

Britain, and Brittany, has yielded stone hammers with transverse grooves for fastening to a haft.

Behrens remarks that the people of the time were quite

unconscious of a revolution in civilization, and this warns us of the unwisdom of maintaining the emphasis formerly placed upon the distinction between Neolithic and Bronze Ages. The *Corridors of Time* have tried to show that diffusions of culture are most complex, and that certain elements of the culture of the ancient lands of the eastern Mediterranean spread in Europe faster than others, the technique of smelting and alloying naturally spreading slowly, because of transport and organization

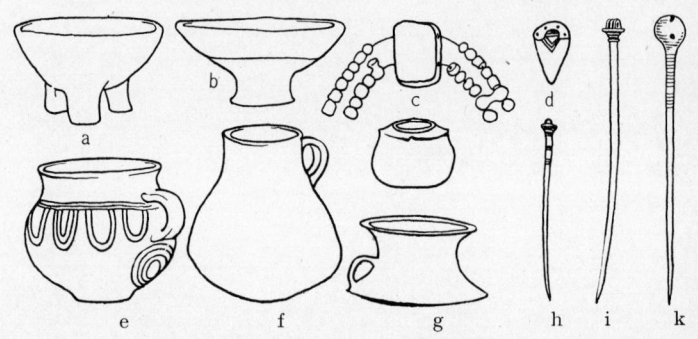

FIG. 19. Early Aunjetitz objects. *a, b, e, f, g*, pots; *c*. amber necklace; *d*. dagger; *h, i, k*. pins.

needed, and probably because of the secretiveness of inventors. The result was that a so-called Neolithic Phase has been recognized for Europe, but it would be more correctly appraised as the herald of the spread of metal. The appreciation of tin as a component of an alloy is thought by Childe to go back to a very early period in Mesopotamia, and a metal bowl of copper with 8·5 per cent. of tin has recently been found in the grave of Shubad at Ur, as mentioned in chapter 2.

Whether Aunjetitz was the first bronze-working site in central Europe or not, it is recognized as a type for the Early Bronze Age in central Europe.

The early or Proto-Aunjetitz phase is largely the same as the

Central Europe

Marschwitz culture already mentioned. The station of Weinzierl known in this connexion has yielded river shells, fish remains, and specimens of common wheat (*Triticum vulgare*) and emmer (*Triticum dicoccum*). Stone-cists and stone-cairns did not occur amongst the oldest graves, but there were cases of cremation in north-west Bohemia, though the general fashion was that of

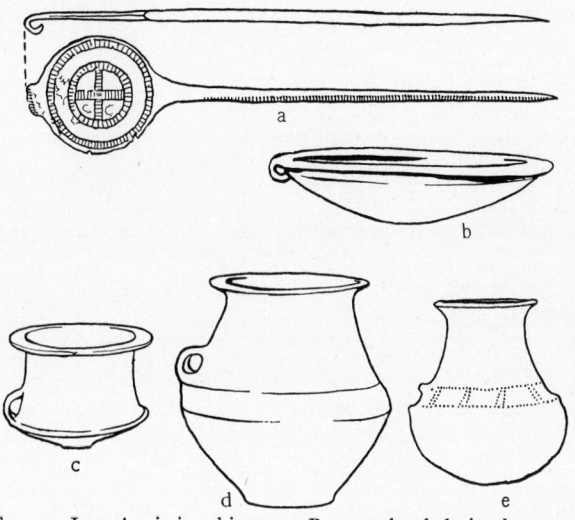

Fig. 20. Late Aunjetitz objects. *a*. Racquet-headed pin; *b–e*, pots.

burying bodies lying on one side with the knees bent up to a variable extent. Sometimes two or more bodies were placed in one grave. The earliest pottery of the Aunjetitz culture has less decoration than that found at Marschwitz. Metal in graves is uncommon, but copper wire and gold wire are known. Good flint work, reminiscent of Baltic coastlands, is found, and a good deal of horn was used.

The Aunjetitz culture proper has an abundance of metal, and pottery is no longer of Marschwitz type. In Bohemia this culture is found north of the rivers Sazawa and Beraun, west of the uppermost Elbe and east of the Biela river. It also occurs in Silesia, especially in Upper Silesia, as in Bohemia chiefly on loess subsoil, though also on black earth patches south of Breslau, in the home-area of the Marschwitz culture. It spread thence northwards into western Poland and the Oder basin. Silesia and Bohemia were linked less through Moravia than through the Glatz district east of the Riesengebirge, for, though western Moravia has many sites of the Aunjetitz group, they are on the lower lands just beneath the hills separating Bohemia from Moravia, west and south-west of Brno (Brünn), and around Olomouc (Olmütz). Some settlements below the little Carpathians are related to both Aunjetitz and Hungary. In Austria the Aunjetitz culture spread from Moravia among the lower hills on the two sides of the Danube below the point of widening of the valley. Upper or western Austria was not affected at this stage. An important further area of Aunjetitz culture was in the Elster-Saale-Elbe basin in northern Thuringia and Saxony. This area has yielded the double-axe in metal and is famed for salt. Childe thinks that corded-ware people formed an aristocracy over an Aunjetitz population, and that Saxony in the Early Bronze Age traded with Britain. This area reaches out towards Weimar and Sondershausen, and may have been linked with Bohemia through the valley of the Eger rather than through that of the Elbe. Outposts in Bavaria near Straubing, between Regensburg and Passau, were probably connected with the Elster-Saale area by way of the Franconian Jura.

The rectangular houses and the villages of the time seem to have been built of wood daubed with clay, but there were some larger fortified settlements, notably at Hradek near Caslau. Common utensils were still largely of stone and bone. Abundant hoards of bronze suggest that little was discarded; it was rather collected up for remelting. One finds flat axes, axes with raised edges, commonly called flanged axes, and large rings for necks and arms. The axes are typically straight-sided with expanded edges curved in a semicircle. Simple daggers are common, and later become curved and ornamented.

Types of metal pins have been used as indices of culture phases, but comparative typology is dangerous here. A pin used to join together two pieces of cloth must have some device to prevent slipping. An expanded head provides this at one end and a bend diminishes the danger at the other. If, however,

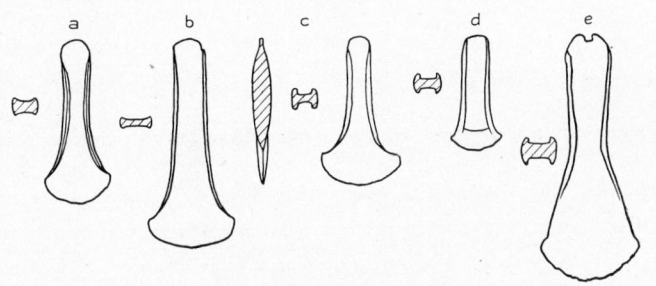

FIG. 21. Various types of flanged axes. *a* and *e*, Switzerland; *b* and *c*, England; *d*, Brittany.

the expanded head be bored and a thread be fastened to it and wound around the other part of the pin, above the bend, there is much greater safety. Some Aunjetitz pins have the head-end curved round and round the axis like a scarf and are thought to be related to those of Hungary, the Aegean and Cyprus; they appear early at Aunjetitz. A round eye typically pierces a widening of the pin-head, or may be on a special expansion inserted into the pin-head. In racquet-pins the head has been hammered out and bent over so that it may catch a thread. The shaft of the pin is sometimes bent and the form and ornamentation of the head vary greatly. Childe notes that some pins have the thread above mentioned replaced by a metal chain.

Ornamental chains in bronze and gold are another feature, while the old habit is continued of making rings of doubly-bent gold wire. This evidence from hoards must be set beside more meagre data from settlements to get a reasonable picture.

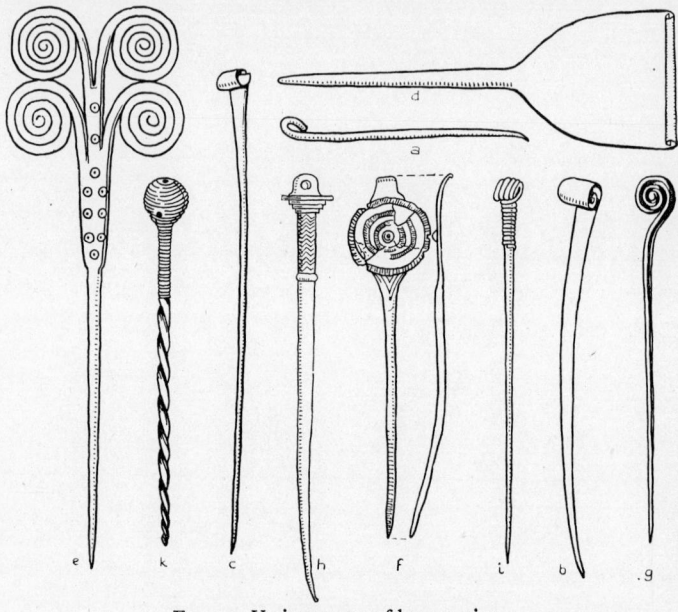

Fig. 22. Various types of bronze pins.

The graves of this culture, from varied beginnings, develop a regular type, probably with a ritual meaning. The knees are bent up towards the skull; the body lies on the right side with the head south and the eyes towards sunrise. It is thought that the corpse was usually covered with wood weighted down by stones, but sometimes stone-cists were used. A supposed link with Aegean culture is an occasional burial in an urn. A pin on the breast is often our only hint of clothing, but fragments of material have been found. Grave furniture is most variable and includes ornaments, notably beads of amber that suggest links with Baltic lands. Marine shells and representations of marine shells in an alloy are other features.

In Silesian stations we have developments from the Marschwitz fashion and incoming influences from Bohemia modifying native style. Technique becomes refined and the ware becomes extremely thin. For Bohemia we may say that, while there is north-western, or at least Thuringian, influence, the eastern Mediterranean, as in the case of the needles, is an important contributor. Gradually the profile of the pots becomes sharper; many pots have the neck portion conical, and the handle at the broad base of the cone; ornamentation is rare, but some pieces show traces of a white incrustation characteristic in Hungary.

Tin, copper, and salt helped the Aunjetitz culture, also a soil often underlain by loess, relatively fertile and open. At first north Bohemia lacked direct connexion both southward and towards Moravia; its individuality has been a marked feature at several periods, including historic times, when it became the highly persistent spring of Czech nationalism.

To the west, in middle and south Germany, and in Burgundian France, earlier civilization persisted with, near the Rhine, beakers and other pots with zoned decoration. Beaker resemblances make Childe think the beaker-making people spread from the Rhine to Britain and eventually left their Rhenish seats, or some of them, to the men of a bronze-using culture. This culture is best seen at Adlerberg near Wörms. Flint tools were still common, but there are simple triangular copper or bronze daggers, rings, and bent pins with the somewhat flattened head bent over to catch the thread. The pottery was rough, sometimes with ornament derived from that of beakers. Objects in ivory and Mediterranean shells, Schumacher thinks, indicate contacts southwards by way of the Rhône valley, but it is questionable whether that valley was fully open to intercourse. The Rhine may have received its early bronze culture from Aunjetitz.

Early Bronze hoards are few in western Germany and eastern France, but a few occur in the loess area of Rhenish Hesse, near Mainz, a region rich in finds of most periods of antiquity. Mound graves characterized middle Germany in the Early Metal Age, and they seem to have spread from middle to south Germany and north-east France. This culture apparently supplanted in some places the Aunjetitz civilization, which had travelled from the west of Bohemia or the Elster-Saale area to Bavaria, where it occurs at Straubing in lower Bavaria and the loess and hill-slopes of south Bavaria, where salt occurs. Bronze Age amber beads give general confirmation here.

Western Germany and north-east France at this time formed one culture province, reaching down the Rhône-Saône basin about as far as Vienne. Between Vienne and Montélimar the Rhône valley is, for the most part, narrow, and there is a noteworthy absence of finds of the Early Bronze Age here. It seems not to have been a line of communication, probably because of dense forest. Farther south, especially east and south-east, we are in a province of culture distinct both from that on the north and from that of the megalithic culture west of the Rhône. Copper in dolmens west of the southern Rhône has been thought to suggest the spread of metal into Burgundy and south Germany from that source, but this is very dubious. The copper-containing dolmens of departments flanking the Rhône basin seem to be a relatively poor and late culture, perhaps persisting until copper beads spread about in western Europe.

South-east of the Rhône megaliths are rarer than anywhere else in France, and the region was early occupied by agriculturists, whom we may suppose received the idea of wheat from central Europe through north Italy or Burgundy. Rock

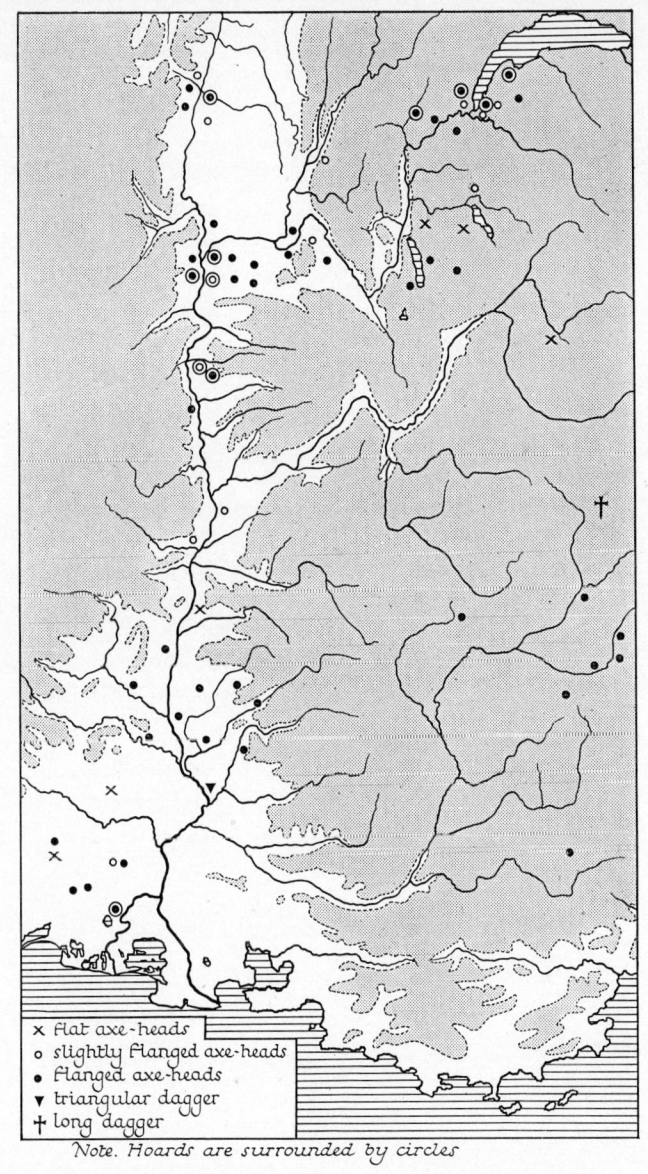

FIG. 23. The Lower Rhône basin in the Early Bronze Age.

engravings of the region of the Col de Tende, with their indisputable representations of ploughs, halberds, and lances, almost

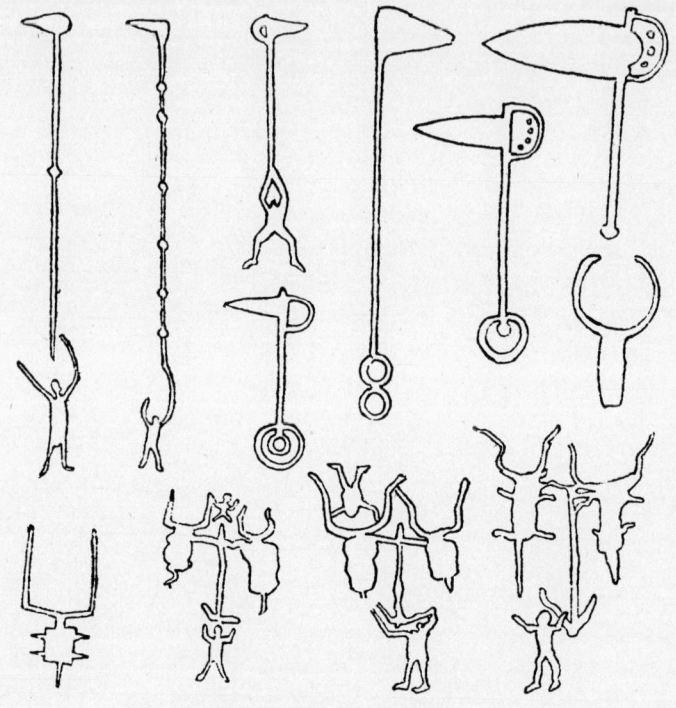

FIG. 24. Rock engravings in the Ligurian Alps.

certainly point to the Bronze Age. The region towards the Rhône yields more of these drawings.

The bronze sickle is found in many places in north Italy, and by far the greater number found in France has come from the Rhône basin, though the department of Jura is far more important than the south-east. These sickles again witness to an agricultural population in the Bronze Age, but neither the drawings nor the sickles may be as early as our period. Déchelette thought that this population might have been the ancestors of the Ligures of later history. He noted that place-names, including the form *asco*, *usco*, and such like, are to be found mainly in the departments of Corsica, Alpes Maritimes, Var, Bouches-du-Rhône, Hérault, Basses Alpes, Hautes Alpes, Drôme, Isère, and Rhône, in Italy north-west of the Arno, and in Switzerland adjacent to Italy—that is to say, in the territory assigned to the Ligures of early history and in that of the culture that we are considering. Links with central Europe enriched this culture, which, Déchelette believed, arose, without great movements, thanks to the veins of tin and copper in the Tuscan Apennines. We may have here another link like those between archaeology and legendary history at Knossos, Troy, and Ur. Déchelette thinks the Ligures themselves traded between north and south. If so, this would help to interpret the rarity in Ligurian territory of both beakers and megaliths, the two main tokens elsewhere of long-distance intercourse in the early age of metal.

The Swiss lake-dwellings long maintained and developed a stone-implement culture, while occasional objects of metal were coming in. The prosperous station of Vinelz used a few copper tools. Fine flint arrow-heads have tangs and barbs, the latter usually parallel to the tang. There are also fine flint knives. Along with these, however, occur perforated battle-axes, evidently related to those of Baltic lands, and a northward cultural link is also indicated by the pottery, akin to corded-ware or *Schnur-keramik*. Flat axes and copper daggers are a feature, and one dagger is of Aegean type with a long tang bent back upon itself to form a hook. The double axe is another important form, found at a number of stations. This Vinelz culture seems to correspond to the three last phases of a scheme of 'Neolithic' culture, worked out for Switzerland by Vouga. Northerly influences in Switzerland at this time were brought by long-headed men, who intruded among the earlier broad heads, but there was no marked revolution.

Ischer found a later culture at Les Roseaux, Morges, and arrow-

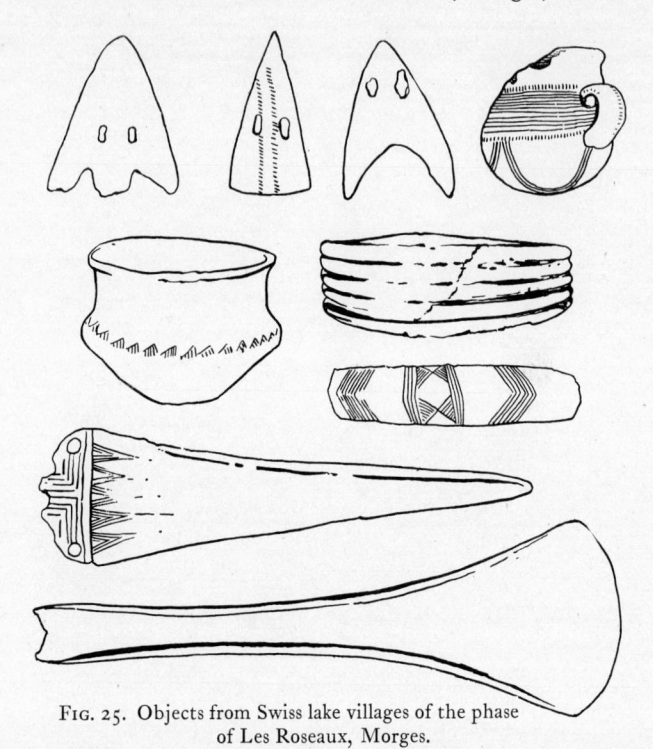

FIG. 25. Objects from Swiss lake villages of the phase of Les Roseaux, Morges.

heads of bronze show that we are dealing with a time after the beginning of the Bronze Age, though stone tools continued to be important until this phase neared its end. Daggers, as well as flat and flanged axes, occur at this stage. It seems that at the close of this phase the Swiss lake-dwellings temporarily diminished in importance or underwent some change preliminary to their redevelopment in the Late Bronze Age, the story of which belongs to our next volume. This change may have been connected with a rise of the levels of the lakes, by which dwellings were flooded out.

On most of the Italian lakes, from Maggiore to Garda, and still farther east in the Veneto, are found villages of pile-dwellings, much like those of Switzerland. These, like their Swiss counterparts, seem to have been erected in the marshes around the lakes; in fact, several have been found in peat-bogs, e.g. at Mercurago and Lagozza, just south of Lago Maggiore. The culture here in so many respects resembles that found in Switzerland that we can hardly doubt the connexion. The Italian series, however, fall into two groups, one extending from Maggiore to Garda, the other in or near the Veneto. Both seem to be of Alpine origin, but to have arrived in Italy by different routes. Simple daggers and axes, both flat and flanged, show that the settlements lasted beyond the Early Bronze Age. That at Peschiera, indeed, seems to have survived into the period during which iron was introduced.

BOOKS

CHILDE, V. GORDON. *Dawn of European Civilization* (London, 1925).
CHILDE, V. GORDON. *The Danube in Prehistory* (Oxford, 1929).
CHILDE, V. GORDON. *The Bronze Age* (Cambridge, 1930).
MYRES, J. L. *Cambridge Ancient History*, vol. i (Cambridge, 1923).

5
The Early Middle Bronze Age in Central Europe

THE last chapter sketched the growth of a bronze-working industrial culture in central Europe, notably in Hungary and Bohemia. Both show a measure of continuity from the introduction of bronze-working right on to the later phases of the

Bronze Age, in which the sword, the socketed axe-head and the safety-pin became widespread, and the rite of cremation for a time replaced that of inhumation as a means of disposing of the dead. We must discuss here the development of bronze culture up to the eve of the introduction of the sword and the other novelties mentioned, developments that give us interesting clues concerning the establishment of new interregional intercourse, destined to have important consequences in later times, and also clues concerning oscillations of climate valuable in interpreting events even beyond the bounds of Europe.

The lake-dwellings of Switzerland declined as the Early Bronze Age drew to a close. Finds attributable to the Middle Bronze Age have been made chiefly near the points where outflowing streams leave those lakes, and it is characteristic that such streams are rapid with a marked slope, so that the lower ends of the lakes are in many cases free from dangers of flooding and have become the sites of such important cities and towns as Geneva, Zürich, and Luzern. Later, there occurs a revival of lake villages, but they decline and disappear in the Early Iron Age through a rise of the levels of the lakes, connected with the oncoming of a cool and wet phase of climate, with which we shall deal in a later volume.

We connect the Early Middle Bronze Age with a phase of rising lake-levels, but that does not necessarily imply cooling or increased rain, as does the similar rise in the Early Iron Age, for the latter is associated with evidences of reduced temperature and increased moisture far and wide. For the Middle Bronze Age the indications are of quite another kind. The south Russian plain, for example, seems to have been almost deserted at this time, and this is the period of the Hyksos domination in Egypt; it is also probably the period of the outpushing of the Aryan-speaking groups from the Asiatic steppe into India, while the legendary history of China tells of horsemen on the

Chinese borders in the late days of the Hsia Dynasty. These data suggest that the continental interior, probably with a fairly large population after a period of prosperity, was pouring out its people during a phase of drought. In the Late Bronze Age the west Baltic obviously had a period of warmth and prosperity, and so had the hill-slopes of Hungary on the east. Both regions declined during the Early Iron Age, and in the west Baltic there is evidence that the oak was then replaced by the beech. Again, in the Middle and Late Bronze Ages, the population in central Europe increased, especially in the valleys. Similarly in the Britain of the Middle Bronze Age the palstave culture spread far and wide, and was followed by a period that does not seem to have been prosperous. The indications are thus that the Middle and Late Bronze Ages were periods of warm and relatively dry conditions. How then may we understand the apparent rise of the lake-levels in Switzerland during the Middle Bronze Age? The most useful hypothesis seems to be one which appreciates the fact that an early result of a rise in temperature near a glaciated mountain-chain is an increased melting of the ice, resulting in a rise of the levels of the lakes fed by the streams descending from the glaciers. Later on an equilibrium would be established, and the glaciers would be much reduced, and evaporation would by this time balance, or more than balance, the water-supply; thus the lake-levels would tend to fall once more rather than to rise.

The villages on the banks of the Tisza in Hungary, which were so important in the Early Bronze Age, seem to have declined for a while before the rich culture of the Hungarian Late Bronze Age blossomed out. We shall not, however, attempt to speculate as to whether this decline was related to the fall of Hissarlik II or to climatic factors.

In Hungary, near the Tisza, the villages just mentioned, and already noticed in the previous chapter, are set on terraces above the flood-level, and the facts concerning them have been collated by Childe. Toszeg, one of these villages, has constructions of horizontal logs within a palisade of piles that bears some resemblance to certain structures found in the Po Basin, to be described later on in this chapter as *Terremare* settlements. The houses were approximately, but not perfectly, rectangular, and the floors were of stamped clay. The settlement was surrounded by a moat or watercourse, probably related to the delta of a tributary stream, the inner bank being supported by piles, which suggest that the village may have been built on an artificial mound, raised to avoid the floods. There seem also to have been pit-dwellings on some Hungarian sites. The pottery of the Early and Middle Bronze Age in Hungary often maintains the old bulb-and-neck form, with details related to those of the Aunjetitz pots; the bronze axe-heads are still for the most part flat, and flat triangular daggers occur. Remains of the horse are common, and an antler cheek-piece of a bit shows that this animal had been domesticated. Childe traces the advent of the domestic horse into east central Europe to an earlier period, in which contacts between the south Russian steppe and Hungary are indicated in the widespread use of ochre in graves and in other ways. Other Hungarian sites, but not the Toszeg of this stage, have yielded animal figurines and types of pottery with a crescent-shaped handle, known in Italy as *ansa lunata*. These have been thought to suggest a close link between Hungary and the Po.

The Early Bronze Age cultures of Hungary and Bohemia had spread in the directions indicated in the last chapter, reaching Moravia and the Viennese Danube, as well as many parts of Germany, including Silesia. Ornaments of the Hungarian Early and Middle Bronze Ages are found fairly widely in Germany and Switzerland. Childe thinks that the Hungarian culture of the Middle Bronze Age also spread up the Tisza valley and across the Carpathians, whence a series of hoards marks a line across Little Poland. It is by this route, rather than through Moravia,

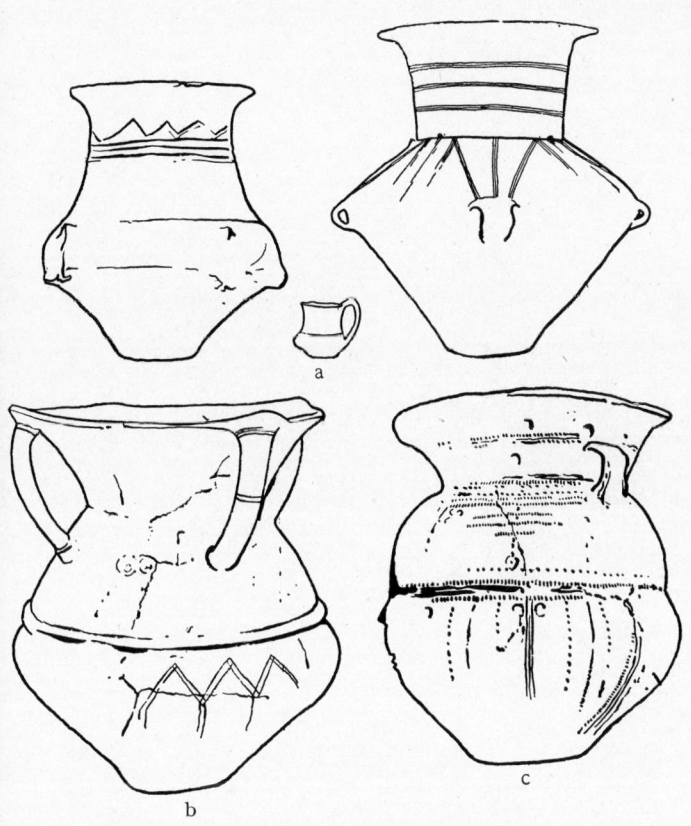

FIG. 26. Early and Middle Bronze Age pots from Hungary. *a*, corded urns, Vatina; *b*, Surčin; *c*, Temes-Kubin. After Childe.

that Hungary and Silesia would seem to have communicated at this time. In some such way there arose an important culture, one centre of which was in Silesia; it is usually known, from the region richest in remains, as the Lausitz culture. The general distribution of this culture is not very different from that of the preceding phase, known as the Aunjetitz, but its interest is greatly enhanced by the fact that, as the middle phase passed into the late phase of the Bronze Age, there grew from it, or from the contemporary Hungarian civilization, or from both, the Urn-fields culture, which will interest us in our next volume. It also has the interest of unfortunate political controversy, various writers having tried to make different prehistoric cultures either proto-Slavonic or proto-Germanic according to taste. The Lausitz culture, for example, has been proclaimed as proto-Slavonic. There is little doubt that Lausitz features linger on into cultures that have the right to be called Slavonic, just as features of this and other cultures linger on into what may be Germanic phases. None the less the antedating of group-names that stir political prejudices is to be deprecated.

The early pots of the Lausitz culture have at the base an inverted cone, above which is a bulbous portion that is sharply marked off from the wide and rather short neck. Either at the junction of bulb and neck, or extending from that junction to the rim, there may be one, two, or four handles. The bulbs are often decorated with *mammae* or warts, typically four, though sometimes six or eight in number, and the edge of the *mamma* is usually marked by incised lines. Some pots have long necks and broad handles, some are rather broad dishes, while others are burial urns of biconical and other forms, which later become very important in the Urn-fields culture.

Burial, at first by inhumation as in the Aunjetitz phase, was superseded in course of time by cremation, the feature of the Urn-fields. Metal is not common in graves of this culture, but some flanged bronze axe-heads are known, and, in some hoards and stray finds, one also gets axe-heads with a transverse ridge or stop-ridge crossing between two median flanges; this is an early form of the palstave. The origin of that implement, however, does not in all probability belong to the Lausitz culture; its early stages will be discussed later in this chapter.

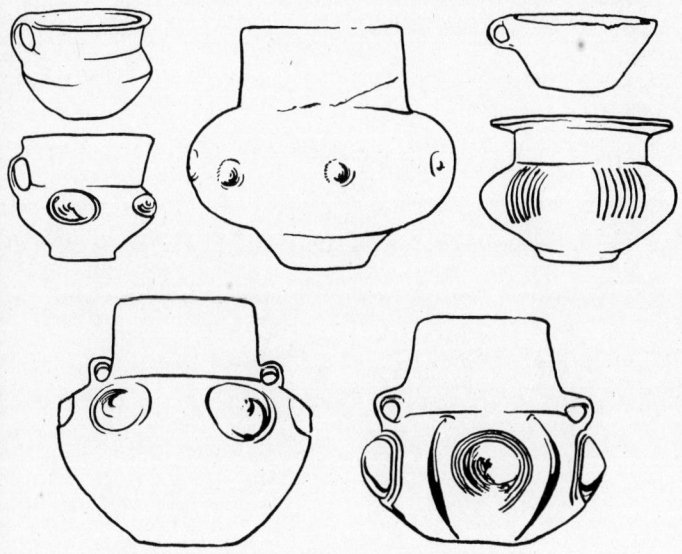

FIG. 27. Early pottery of the Lausitz culture.

In Germany, west of Silesia, there seem also to have lived during the Middle Bronze Age scattered peoples who buried their dead on the uplands, and this is characteristic of this period in England and Wales as well. The body was usually laid on the earth or on a slab, and a mound of stones and earth was piled over it; these people did not dig graves. Often the stones over the body were arranged to form a chamber, and very often a husband and wife were buried together, giving evidence of monogamy. Several barrows often occur near one another, but there are no evidences of large communities such as we get later.

It seems probable that these people of the barrows or tumuli, as they are often called, were herdsmen of the uplands, who may have overlapped the valley dwellers of the next succeeding period. The evidence of special occupation of the uplands seems, so far as it goes, an indication of dry conditions of climate. British archaeologists, and notably E. T. Leeds, have recently gathered evidence to show that in England, from the dawn of the Metal Age onwards, there have been valley settlements, especially on gravel benches, as at Abingdon, more or less contemporary with other settlements on the uplands. It is interesting to speculate on the possibility of these having been the original nuclei of some of the valley villages in Britain, which have so widely been thought to date only from Anglo-Saxon times.

The specialization of parts of the bronze axe-head must next be argued. At first the bronze or copper axe-head was only a slightly adapted version of its stone predecessor, but thinner, because metal was less likely to crack and the material was doubtless scarce, while the edge tended to expand as the result of being hammered out. In the Aunjetitz culture, especially, the cutting-edge was often expanded into a semicircle. The typical method of hafting was by pressing the butt end of the axe-head into a split, and often bent, stick, and this was another reason for thinness. Axe and split stick were then bound together by cord or wire. Nevertheless the axe-head must have tended to slip and the stick to split farther along. These two difficulties were met in different ways. The slipping of the axe-head from side to side was checked by the development of flanges, which, in Saxony, Bohemia, and Silesia, were developed in many cases along a narrow and medially narrowing stem of an axe with a broad semicircular cutting-edge. In other types, specially abundant in north-western Germany and Hesse, the edge, though curved, is less expanded, and the stem is broader, and, in some of them, the flange is specially developed about the middle of the axe-head. This kind of development continued in two diverging ways. In central and south Germany the median portion of the flange was expanded on each side into wings that curved round the ends of the hafting stock and so held it in place. Thus arose the winged axe-head, highly characteristic of the Middle Bronze Age in central Europe. On the other hand, in north-west Germany, and to a certain extent in Hesse and Alsace, as well as here and there in the main areas

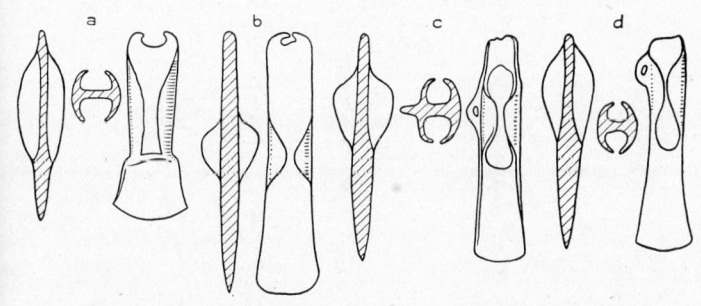

FIG. 28. Winged bronze axe-heads. *a, b*, Italy; *c, d*, Switzerland.

of the winged axe-head, the median flanges were linked by a ridge across the blade, making a stop beyond which the split stick could not be pushed. This type of axe-head with a thin blade-butt, median flanges, and a stop-ridge on each face, is called the palstave. Its importance in the Middle Bronze Age in Britain is remarkable and suggests, as do so many other features, that Britain was at that time related in life especially to lands across the North Sea.

Childe thinks the palstave Rhenish, Breuil thought it western, Lissauer suggested north German origins. Sometimes, especially in Bohemia and the Baltic, axe-heads were made long and narrow, and a bronze collar, imitating and doubtless replacing a cord or wire binding, was added near the butt end to strengthen the hafting.

To return to the culture of the German barrows, one finds in them a good many ornaments related to those of Hungary, and Hungarian fashions penetrated even into Bohemia. There are also short daggers with rivet-holes at the butt-end, and longer weapons called rapiers or dirks, the predecessors of the sword, but not yet long enough to deserve that name.

There seems no doubt that a good deal of the culture of the Early and Middle Bronze Ages in South and West Germany developed among descendants of the tumulus-builders, who had made cord-ornamented pottery, known in Germany as *Schnurkeramik*, and while they acquired some of the ideas of the Lausitz culture they developed several local variants before metal reached them. Apparently they picked up a good deal of their metallurgy from Hungary rather than from Aunjetitz, while other ideas came in with amber traders, whose routes through south Germany increased considerably in the Middle Bronze Age. The main route from Jutland followed the Elbe to Bohemia, which it crossed to reach the Danube, but another route along the Saale valley became important in due course and branched in south Germany. These routes converged upon the Inn valley and used the Brenner pass on the way to the Adige and the Adriatic. East Baltic amber may have been known at this time but its importance developed in the Late Bronze Age. The amber routes seem to have been the main lines of intercourse in Europe at the time and exchanges along them are important helps in dating phases of the Bronze Age civilization. Amber beads are found in Bohemia and adjacent parts of Germany already in Early Bronze Age graves.

The tumulus culture, which spread in west Hungary, overlapped its predecessor, the Aunjetitz culture, but the latter was better developed in the valleys, while the former was essentially of the hills. It seems also to have lasted on into the period of the Urn-fields culture which followed it; that,

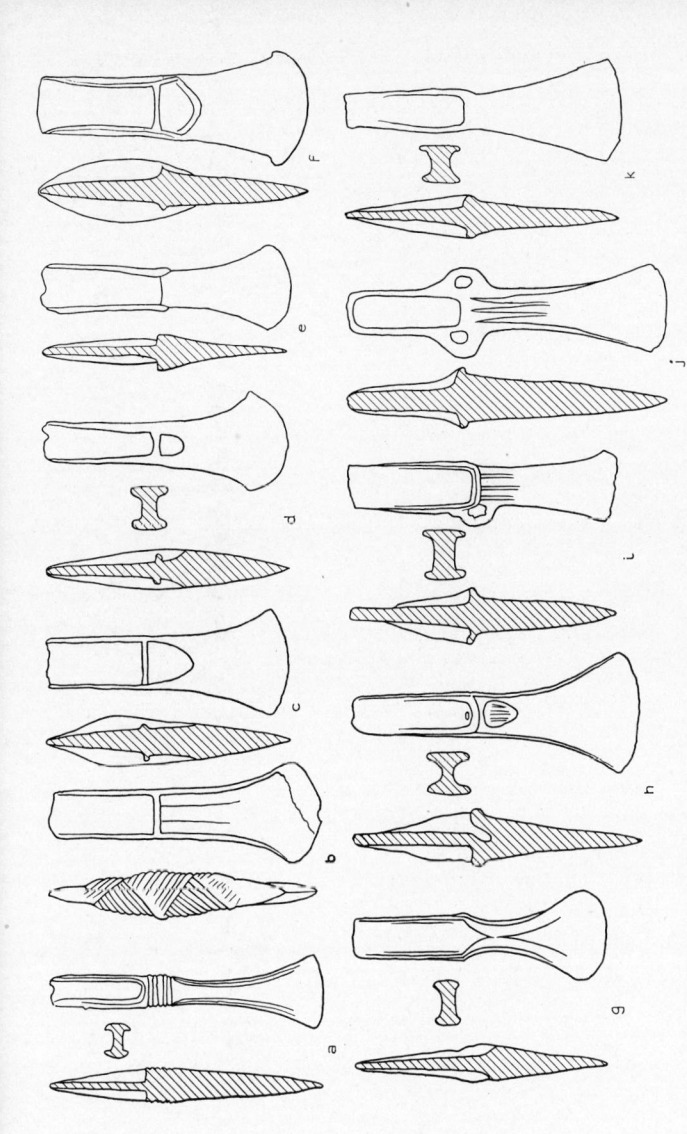

FIG. 29. Bronze palstaves. *a.* Denmark; *b.* Brittany; *c.* Hungary; *d.* Italy; *e.* Germany; *f.* France; *g.* Hungary; *h.* England; *i.* Switzerland; *j.* Spain; *k.* England.

however, was again a culture, to a large extent, of the lower lands. *The Way of the Sea*, p. 24, noticed episodes in the story of the south Russian steppe and the Black-earth lands to its north-west. We suggested that early settlements in that region had been destroyed by steppe-nomads about 2600 B.C. At Cucuteni, at Tripolje near Kiev, and in eastern Galicia there arose later a second series of settlements, usually with painted pottery, but also some decorated with incised ornament in the Ukraine; at Bilcze Złota a flat copper dagger has been found. This village life continued during the Early and Middle Bronze Ages, and pots with mammillated bulbous sections, together with hammer-headed pins, tell of cultural links with Hungary and perhaps with Bohemia. The period is not represented by graves in the Russian steppe itself, probably, as stated above, because of the dry climate. The steppe again becomes important in the Early Iron Age, because of the presence of the Scythians, and we know that that was a period with a relatively cool, wet climate.

The region between Hungary and Italy was occupied in the Early and Middle Bronze Ages by cultures showing survivals from that of the Danubian peasants and other adjacent folk; and stray finds indicate exchanges with Italy and Hungary. Figurines from Ljubljana (Laibach) connect the culture there with that of south-west Russia of an earlier period, and the pottery there shows analogous relations. A culture partly Hungarian and partly Alpine spread late in the Early Bronze Age to the Po basin, where there arose the *Terremare*.

A *terramara* has sometimes been called a lake-dwelling on dry land. It was a settlement, somewhat trapezoidal in shape, supported on piles and enclosed by a rampart of earth, outside which was a ditch or moat, fed with water from a running stream. The name is derived from that used locally for the soil of the mounds left by these settlements, which has been carted away for fertilizing the fields. These settlements occur most

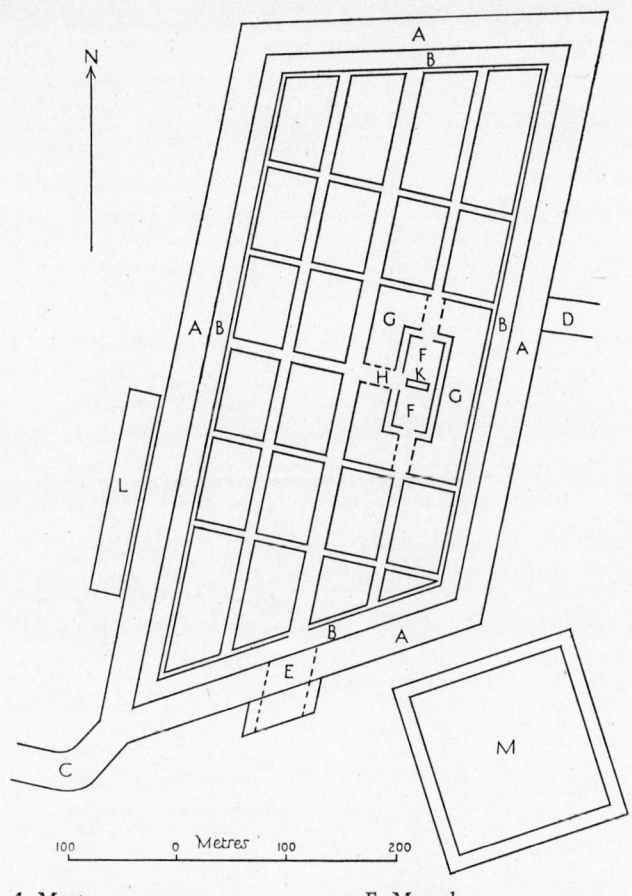

A. Moat.
B. Rampart.
C. Trench supplying moat.
D. Trench draining moat.
E. Bridge.
F. Mound.
G. Moat.
H. Bridge.
K. Trench with Roman tiles.
L, M. Cremation cemeteries.

FIG. 30. Plan of Terramara of Castellazzo. After Pigorini.

plentifully in the province of Emilia, on both sides of the railway between Piacenza and Bologna; others have been noted near Mantua and a few in the provinces of Brescia and Cremona. Remains similar to those in the *terremare* come from the neighbourhood of Verona, while late examples of this culture have been discovered near Taranto, and, it has been thought, at Rome.

A number of bronze implements have been found in the *terremare*, though never in such a way as to enable us to divide this civilization into successive phases. Most of the axes are flanged, of that narrow variety usual in Italy and in some parts of central Europe. These flanged axes in the west are of the close of the Early Bronze Age, but this type persisted later in Italy. Occasionally we find these flanges only in the centre of the sides and developed into wings. The winged-axe lasts on through the Late Bronze Age, and the *terramara* culture, which had them and also swords, may well have lasted even into the Iron Age. The bronze sickle is familiar in *terramara* collections, as it is among those from the region of the supposed early Ligurians discussed in the previous chapter. Daggers, some leaf-shaped with a tang and some triangular with a broad base, are other features, and the bronze pins include a double-headed type, the heads being spiral as in some pins from the Aegean. The tin and copper ores of the Tuscan Apennines became important as the *terremare* developed.

The pottery found in the *terremare* is of two types, both, apparently, contemporary. The ordinary ware was rough, and has been found mostly in the cemeteries. The finer ware, of good grey clay, is dark with a highly polished surface. The majority of the finer pots are bowls, hemispherical, ovoid or biconical, or cups provided with handles, usually with a crescent-shaped terminal, known as the *ansa lunata*. Both types of pottery were hand-made, and the potter's wheel was unknown. Rough figurines of men and animals, some representing pigs, have the surface unpolished. Beads of amber have been found on several sites, and at Montale two of glass paste, possibly imported from the Aegean.

The figurines of animals suggest that they kept these domesticated, while in addition to wild fruits, such as filberts, acorns,

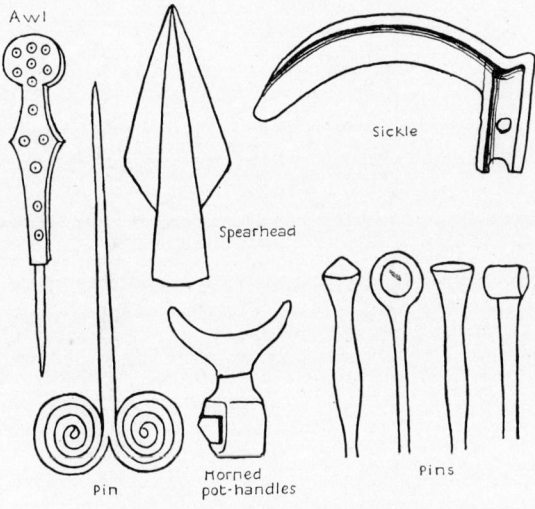

FIG. 31. Objects from the *Terremare*.

wild apples, pears, and cherries, the inhabitants cultivated two varieties of bread-wheat, the vine, beans, and flax.

At Castellazzo two cemeteries were found, both of which are considered to have belonged to the inhabitants of the *terremare* there. One of these showed that the dead were burned and the ashes deposited in urns, covered with inverted basins, and laid close together on a small pile structure resembling a small *terramara*.

The *terremare* for the most part lie clustered thickly on the plain south of the Po between the Trebbia and the Panaro, while a few have been found on either side of the Mincio just south of the Lago di Garda. Some elements of their civilization spread a little farther, for the lake village at Peschiera was much influenced by it, as were settlements nearer Venice.

Among these and to the east, and between them and the Apennines, occur some villages of different type, having round huts, sunk slightly in the earth, and evidently the abodes of the descendants of the earlier population. Some *terramara* pottery has been found in these, but the wares are usually rougher and more primitive. A few flanged axes and other implements of bronze have been found in these huts, but metal was relatively scarce. The invaders were the more advanced of the two populations, which long lived side by side.

BOOKS

CHILDE, V. GORDON. *Dawn of European Civilization* (London, 1925).
CHILDE, V. GORDON. *The Danube in Prehistory* (Oxford, 1929).
CHILDE, V. GORDON. *The Bronze Age* (Cambridge, 1930).
MYRES, J. L. *Cambridge Ancient History*, vol. i (Cambridge, 1923).
PEET, T. E. *Stone and Bronze Ages in Italy* (Oxford, 1909).
FOX, C. *Archaeology of the Cambridge Region* (Cambridge, 1923).
British Museum Guide to the Bronze Age.

6

The Middle Bronze Age in West and South-West Europe

OUR second chapter referred to the poor evidence for the Bronze Age in the Iberian peninsula after the initial phase; until towards its close the implements show little change in form and are not common. Tin-streaming there may have ceased to be remunerative, though fresh discoveries, perhaps in the north-west of the peninsula, may cause a change of view. On the basis of our interpretation of the dolmens of north-west Spain as late compared with the more elaborate examples farther south, as given in *The Way of the Sea*, chapter 3, it is possible to think of activity continuing fairly late in Spanish Galicia; and it is interesting in this connexion to recall the view that the famous cult of Santiago da Compostella in Galicia seems to be based on the veneration of megaliths.

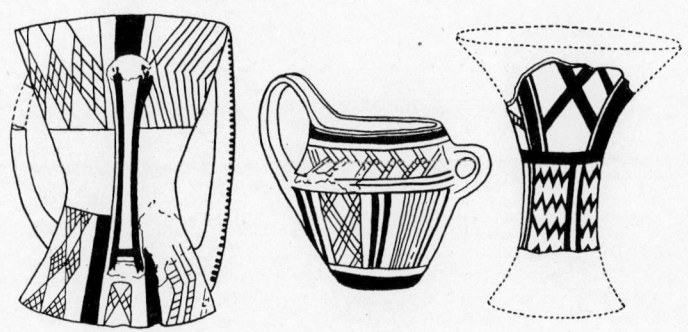

FIG. 32. Pottery of the First Siculan period.

The depressed state of civilization noted in the Iberian peninsula was also a feature of Sicily, at this time passing from its first Siculan period, characterized by pottery ornamented with designs in black on a red ground, to its Second Siculan phase, which must have begun soon after bronze was introduced, and which lasted until after 1200 B.C. This period gives plain unpainted pottery, with grey or yellow surface, usually ornamented with incised designs. Nearly all the numerous cemeteries belong to the later part of the period, after the final destruction of the Palace of Knossos. Some of the tombs at Milocca may, it is true, go back to 1450 B.C., but the only earlier cemetery appears to be that at Plemmirio, just across the harbour from Syracuse. Here tombs are cut in rock at the base of a shaft, from which a small door or window leads into a circular burial chamber, sometimes with a flat roof, more often with a dome suggestive of a *tholos*. Around the chamber are a number of niches, cut in the rock, while beneath is often a rough bench, cut in the rock against the wall, a feature, as Hemp has shown, of tombs of the early days of metal in the Balearic Islands.

A number of bodies was placed in each tomb, showing that the custom of communal burial still survived. Among objects found here was a quantity of grey pottery, incised with typical Second Siculan decoration, an obsidian knife, beads of glass, bronze, bone, and some resinous substance, and a comb of bone or ivory. A bronze rapier, of eastern Mediterranean type, and a sword both seem to be slightly later, showing that the tombs continued to be used after 1400 B.C.

In south Italy the inhabitants continued to live in circular huts, with floors sunk a few feet in the ground; in this respect they were carrying on a neolithic custom. Three rock-cut tombs have been found at Matera, two of which may date from this time. The few bronze implements found seem to have been imported from the north of the peninsula.

If there is ground for the suggestion made in chapter 4 that the Middle Bronze Age was a period of warm and rather dry climate this may be a reason for the relative poverty of the cultures of that time in south-west Europe, where, obviously, settlements were still of relatively simple types and men were for the most part at a cultural level which kept them in fairly close dependence on circumstances round about them. The probable exhaustion of remunerative tin-sands in parts of Spain, and the lack of tin in Sicily and south Italy, would be additional factors of this poverty, which would also serve as a temporary check on commerce from the Aegean, a fact mentioned in the next chapter. It is true that not till a later phase of the Bronze Age do we get evidence of decline in Crete, but, on the one hand, that island had highly organized societies less dependent on circumstances, and, on the other hand, that mountainous district may well have retained a water-supply sufficiently organized for the needs of a well-established civilization.

Just as in the Iberian peninsula, so also in Brittany there is doubt as to whether the region maintained its importance as the Bronze Age advanced. Its soils did not lend themselves to agriculture except near the sea, where they could be fertilized with sea-weed, and limed with shell-debris. Moreover, maritime intercourse with the Iberian peninsula had seriously diminished. As the tin-sands of Brittany were of only moderate extent it is likely that they, too, were becoming exhausted. It was in the age of the flat copper axe, and probably just before this, that the maritime intercourse with Spain and Portugal had been important. The flanged axe is rare in the Iberian peninsula; it is, however, important near Breton and Norman coasts, and hoards containing axes of this type are particularly notable in the department of Gironde.

In *The Way of the Sea*, chapter 6, we referred to elaborate monuments, with strong evidence of maritime intercourse, in the vicinity of Arles and Collorgues, Gard, and at Pouy de la Halliade on the plateau north of the Pyrenees. We are inclined to think that the megalithic culture of north-east Spain on the one hand, and of the Cevenol and the Causses departments of France on the other, may represent spreads of ideas on both flanks of that zone of intercourse into regions of relative poverty, which were not greatly encumbered with forest.

Of the hoards of the Bronze Age in southern France, which contain flanged axes and no axes of more elaborate types, two have been found in the department of Gard, one in Hérault, one in Aveyron, one in Ariège, and seventeen in Gironde. Flanged axes have also been found at three places in Ardèche, two in Drôme, five in Gard, and four in Vaucluse, and doubtless at many other places in departments farther west, of which we lack details. Flanged axes with a few palstaves accompanying them occur in several other hoards in some of the departments named, and in that of Dordogne. There is, therefore, good

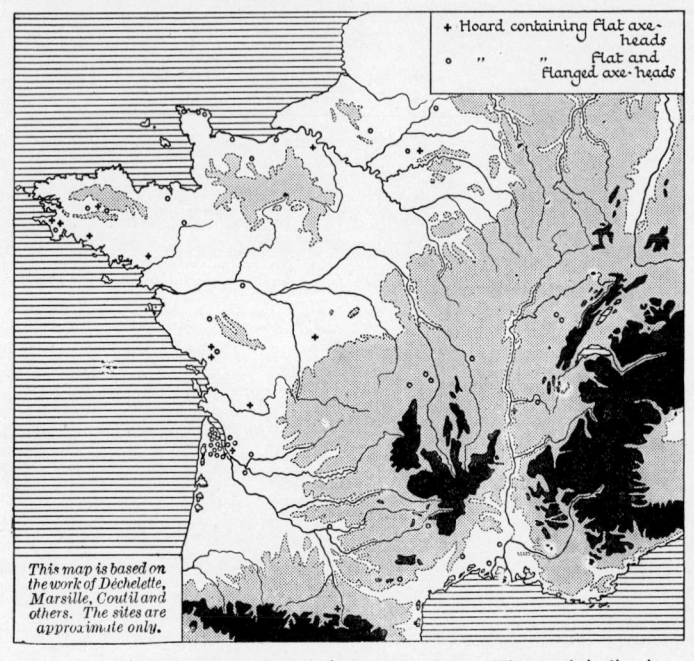

FIG. 33. Early Bronze Age hoards in France. Note. The mark indicating a hoard shows the most advanced axe-type it contains.

reason to suppose that the idea of the flanged axe passed west across southern France, especially if we realize that the type is almost absent from Portugal and rare in Spain.

As the dolmens of the Cevenol region have also yielded some pins of bronze, which clearly represent elements of the Aunjetitz culture brought west, and as the fundamental associations of the flanged axe seem to be with central Europe rather than with Atlantic France, we think that the idea of the flanged axe, with various accompanying ideas of metal ornament, spread to the Atlantic coast of France across the south of that country. It did not reach the south of France down the Rhône, for there is a region between Vienne and, approximately, Montélimar which is remarkably poor in Early Bronze Age remains, and may have been thickly forested at the time; but it may have spread along the Jura and the calcareous mountain zone, generally relatively free from forest-obstruction, though full of difficult slopes, or it may have come through north Italy.

Whatever may have been the state of affairs while both Bohemia and the Iberian peninsula were busy with the beginnings of metallurgy, it is clear that, while civilization in the peninsula was declining, probably because tin-streaming in several areas no longer paid, the primacy remained for a time in central Europe. But for the finding of the pins mentioned above, one might entertain the idea of the independent evolution of the flange of the bronze axe in different regions.

In the last chapter reference was made to the development of the palstave, known in France as *hache-à-talon*.

Palstaves soon ousted other types of axes throughout large parts of Europe, especially in north Germany, Scandinavian countries, and the British Isles. Their form was being improved continually, and loops were added to the sides, through which could be passed thongs, used to affix them more securely to the shafts. They are the characteristic implements of the Middle Bronze Age. They are common in western but not in eastern France, along with other types, during the first phase of the Late Bronze Age. They were never generally adopted throughout France, they are rare or non-existent in Italy, while they reached Spain only in small numbers towards the close of the period, and, at the very end of it, Portugal, where a special type arose with a loop on either side. This type, as Crawford has shown, spread from Portugal to the Atlantic shores of France, to Ireland, and to south-west England.

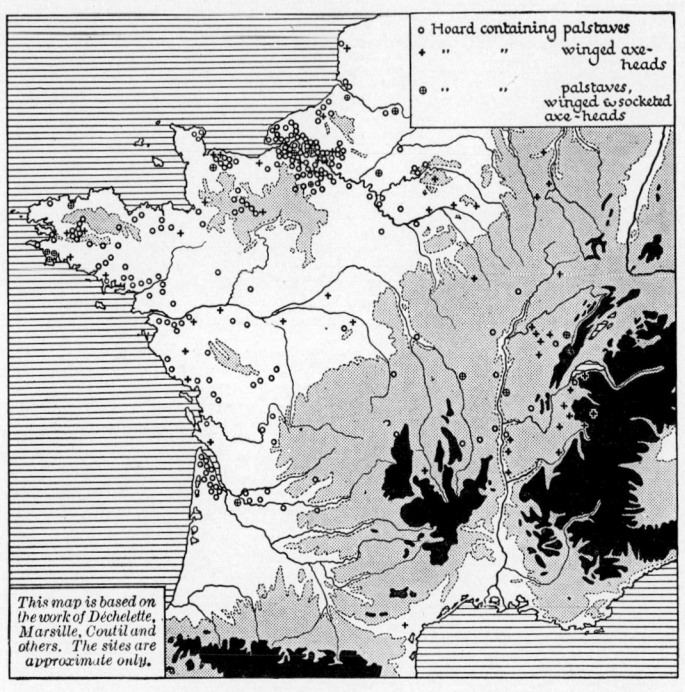

FIG. 34. Middle Bronze Age hoards in France. The mark indicating a hoard shows the most advanced axe-type it contains.

In 1910 Déchelette published a list of the hoards of bronze implements recorded as having been found in France up to that date. Unfortunately in some cases he was unable to specify the types of axes in these hoards, so they cannot all be referred to their proper phase; this is the case with large numbers found in Normandy. Those containing palstaves but no socketed axes have an instructive distribution. They are found near the coast, from the mouth of the Somme to Finistère, especially near the lower Seine and Bayeux, also near the shores of the Bay of Biscay as far south as the mouth of the Garonne. They have also been discovered up the Seine some distance above Paris, a short way up the Loire, right up the Sèvres, and also west of the estuary of the Garonne. Besides these in coastal regions a few have been found in the Saône basin and seven in the upper basin of the Loire. No hoards of this kind have been found near the Mediterranean coast. The great majority of these implements must have arrived by sea, either direct from the Baltic region or from England, while a few have filtered in through the pass of Belfort from the Rhine valley or to the Rhône from Switzerland. The map of Middle Bronze Age hoards in France shows the spread through that country from the east of the winged axe discussed in the last chapter as characteristic of central Europe.

In contrast with what occurred in Brittany, there was a marked development of activity in Ireland, Britain, and Denmark, a development that seems to have led to independent inventions in each country, followed by mutual exchanges. It is interesting to note that in cultural relations, from the dawn of the Metal Age up to the twentieth century of our era, the British Isles have, as it were, swung on the point of Cap Gris Nez, at one time inclining to the northern, in later times Germanic, at others to the southern, afterwards Gallic, side. In the beaker phase, the links had been northerly, and in the megalithic phase more southerly. In the Middle Bronze Age they were mainly northerly again, but the more southerly influences reasserted themselves in a late phase of the Bronze Age, when Brittany, especially the northern half of that province, became very important as the western part of a cultural district stretching along the shores of the English Channel.

The reasons for the importance of the Irish-British-Danish

culture area during the Middle Bronze Age seem to be varied. There was the gold of Ireland, and doubtless to some extent its copper, there were the tin and copper of Cornwall, there were the agricultural possibilities of the chalk and limestone areas of England, especially in what was probably a relatively warm, dry period, and there was the amber of the west Baltic shores. There was also the possibility of maritime intercourse, supplemented, as we think, by land routes across Great Britain, until, during a late phase of the Bronze Age, the sea-route round the north of Scotland, past the Hebrides, came again into use. For, towards the end of the Middle Bronze Age, there occurred a great advance in the civilization of the west Baltic region and its maritime and transcontinental links. A number of objects found there suggest that the people of this area had close trade relations with the people of the Aunjetitz culture of Bohemia, sending amber to them and receiving in return tin and copper from the mines of the Erzgebirge; but this is a subject that must be postponed to our next volume.

There is a great need for a more intensive study of the distribution of the types and subtypes of the bronze implements in use at this time and during the other phases of the Bronze Age. This has been carried out for some years past for the British Isles under the auspices of the British Association for the Advancement of Science, but it needs to be followed up on an international scale before far-reaching conclusions can be drawn. The British catalogue now contains details of nearly 15,000 metal objects of the Bronze Age, including full-size drawings with complete information as to the site and circumstances of their discovery as well as bibliography. The catalogue is now all but complete for the specimens in museums and private collections in England, Wales, the Channel Islands, and the Isle of Man.

The palstave was the typical axe in use in the British Isles

West and South-West Europe

during the Middle Bronze Age, but there have been few specimens found there to indicate the early stages in its evolution, though, as we have seen, the first symptom of the stop-ridge may be noticed in some of the flanged axes in the hoards found at Plymstock and Arreton Down.

During the Middle Bronze Age the daggers grew longer and

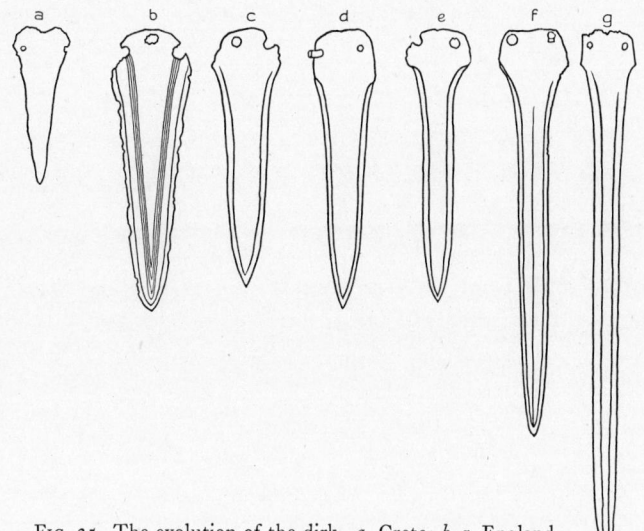

FIG. 35. The evolution of the dirk. *a*, Crete; *b–g*, England.

narrower and the number of rivets fewer. At first the blade had a somewhat ogival outline, as was, indeed, apparent at the close of the Early Bronze Age. Then the butt grew narrower, the rivets were reduced to four and the sides became parallel for the greater part of the length. Thus the dagger of the Early Bronze Age developed into the dirk. As the Middle Bronze Age progressed these dirks grew in length until they became so long as to be known as rapiers; they are not, however, in the least like true rapiers, and since form does not change and every degree of length has been found it is best to call them all dirks. These dirks were thrusting weapons and were too weak at the junction of the blade and the hilt to be used profitably for cutting; slashing swords did not come into use at this time, and their invention and spread throughout Europe ushered in the Late Bronze Age.

One of the great features of the Middle Bronze Age was the spear-head, and this seems to have been specially important in

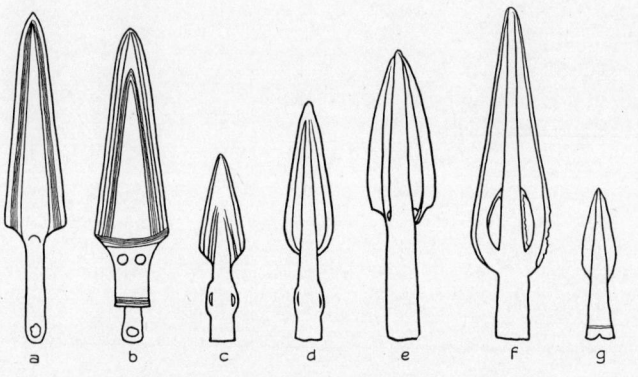

FIG. 36. The evolution of the spear-head in England.

Britain. Simple spears had been known from the earliest days of metal, but these had been flat and, in western Europe, attached to the shaft by a long tang, often containing a loop or eye, through which a rivet could be passed. The primitive spear of Europe was, in fact, a dagger set on the end of a shaft with the axes of both in line, while the halberd was a similar dagger set on with its axis at right-angles to that of the shaft.

Only very few of these early spear-heads have been found in the British Isles, but some of these have been discovered with interesting associations. Thus at Arreton Down one was found with a ferrule of bronze, which had been fixed with rivets round the head of the shaft to prevent it from breaking off when the spear-head struck something heavily. In the same hoard was found another spear-head in which the ferrule, rivet-heads and all, had been cast in one piece with the spear-head, and from that time on we have a steady evolution in the form of the spear-head, continuing right through the Middle Bronze Age; this has been well worked out by Canon Greenwell. The next types had well-defined sockets with loops on either side, through which thongs could be run to tie the spear-head more firmly on to its shaft. By degrees the spear-heads grew longer and more elaborate in section and the loops moved higher and higher up the socket, till at the close of the Middle Bronze Age they formed part of the base of the blade.

BOOKS

CHILDE, V. GORDON. *Dawn of European Civilization* (London, 1925).
CHILDE, V. GORDON. *The Danube in Prehistory* (Oxford, 1929).
CHILDE, V. GORDON. *The Bronze Age* (Cambridge, 1930).
MYRES, J. L. *Cambridge Ancient History*, vol. i (Cambridge, 1923).
PEET, T. E. *Stone and Bronze Ages in Italy* (Oxford, 1909).
FOX, C. *Archaeology of the Cambridge Region* (Cambridge, 1923).
British Museum Guide to the Bronze Age.

7
The Aegean in the Early Bronze Age

ABOUT 2000 B.C. Crete entered its Second Middle Minoan period. This was a time of great prosperity, and owing to its central position the merchant princes of Knossos and Phaestos were carrying on a brisk oversea trade with Egypt, Syria, Asia Minor, Greece, south Italy, and Sicily, while Cretan goods were being carried as far as Spain and Portugal, if not farther to the West.

About 1900 B.C. the Palace of Knossos was remodelled, on a

much larger scale, and the Palace of Phaestos was enlarged at about the same time. Both palaces were built around central courtyards and contained a very large number of rooms; they were fitted with many conveniences of a surprisingly modern appearance, including bathrooms, drains, and water-pipes, with well-fitted sockets. The courts and passages were paved with slabs, sometimes hexagonal and sometimes irregular in shape, of a type used in much later days by the Turks and known as 'mosaiko'. Besides private and public apartments, there were workshops and vast rows of storehouses, as well as shrines or temples. Every aspect of public as well as private life had its appropriate room, and it has been suggested that the rulers or kings, who erected and occupied these vast buildings, were not only kings but also priests and merchants. Whether these two palaces were the abodes of rival monarchs, or the northern and southern residences of the same king, is uncertain, but the balance of evidence seems to be in favour of the existence of two potentates.

The pottery in use during this period was some of the finest ever made in the island. Much of it was so thin as to deserve the name of 'egg-shell' pottery, and it was decorated in several colours, usually white, red and orange on a black ground. This is the well-known polychrome pottery, called Kamares ware from the site at which it was first found. This ware is usually in the form of cups or bowls, but besides these there were *rhytons*, or drinking-horns, decorated with bulls' heads, and large painted jars or *pithoi*, with designs of cords around them, some standing as high as a man; these seem to have been used for storing and shipping oil, which was one of the chief articles of export.

Towards the close of this century we notice a decline in the quality of the pottery, for metal was becoming increasingly used for cups and other vessels. The pottery was now often

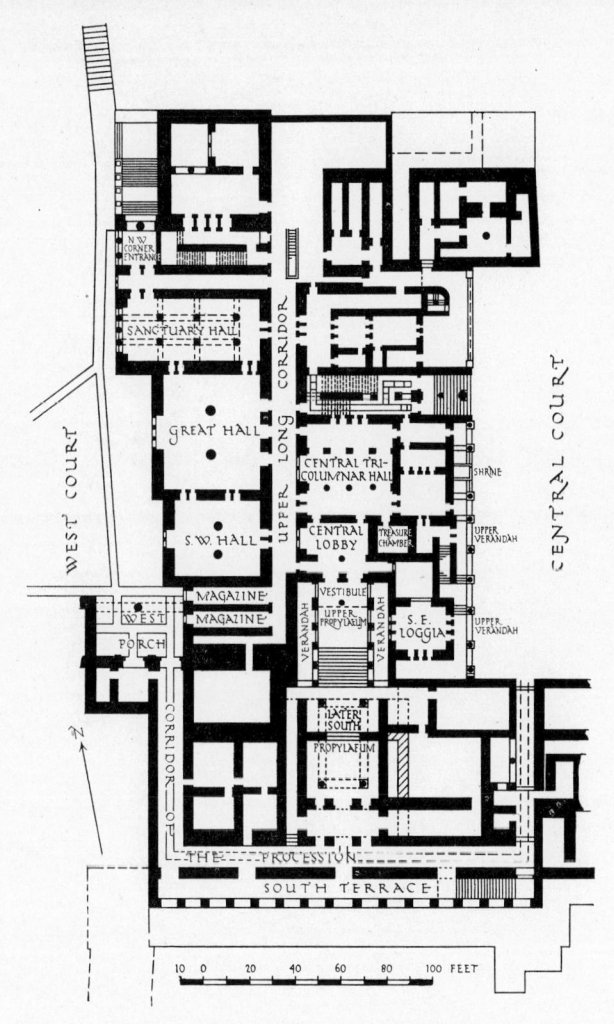

FIG. 37. Plan of the Palace of Knossos.

made of stamped ware, imitating metal originals; and still further to resemble their prototypes these were often painted so as to give a metallic lustre. It is a common feature, noted in other cultures elsewhere, that the potter's art declines when metal comes into general use for domestic purposes.

About 1800 B.C. 'egg-shell' ware ceased to be made, for cups of the precious metals were coming still more into general use, but some were made of a combination of pottery and metal; one has been found made of faience inlaid with gold. Pottery was used only for meaner purposes, and became heavier with coarser materials. About this time the quick potter's wheel seems to have been introduced, mass production became general, and the industry became commercialized. Polychrome decoration grew rarer, and there was a tendency to make pots with a simple dull white decoration on a dark ground. The designs became more conventional and less naturalistic, though the light decoration on the dark ground persisted throughout the whole of the period.

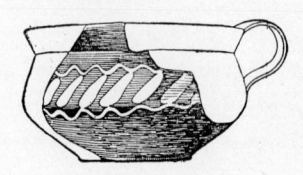

FIG. 38. Pottery imitating metal originals.

Seals, sometimes engraved with the portraits of important people, were a great feature of this period. There was also developed a kind of writing, resembling the hieroglyphic script of Egypt, some of the signs of which had been borrowed from that country. This had been in use during the previous period, and perhaps earlier still, but it was at this time that it became more generally adopted. One interesting feature of this time was the production of miniature copies of buildings in terracotta and faience; these represent the fronts of houses and sometimes shrines, and give us much insight into the domestic and religious architecture of the period.

The Aegean in the Early Bronze Age

Tools were made of bronze. There were double axes, often with one edge as an axe and the other as an adze. Daggers were triangular, sometimes with flat blades and at others with central ribs; these blades tended to get longer and narrower as the period advanced.

As was the case in the previous period, the bodies of the dead were often buried in large jars. The body was placed in a grave in a seated position, with the knees drawn up to the chin, and

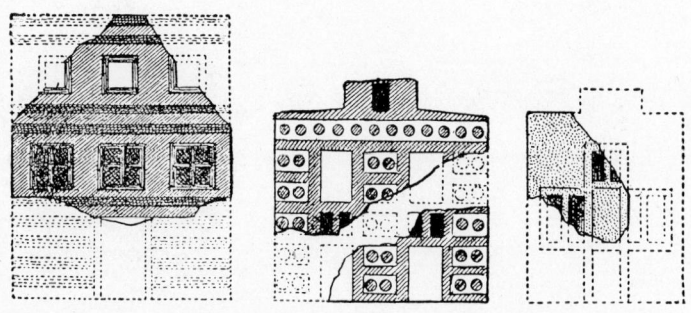

FIG. 39. Faience plaques representing Cretan houses.

then covered with a large jar, after which the grave was filled in with earth.

As we have seen, trade was active during the whole of this period. Much of it was with Egypt, which was flourishing under the rule of the kings of the 12th and 13th Dynasties, generally known as the Middle Kingdom, an account of which has been given in the preceding volume of this series. The Cretans sent wine, oil, and purple dye, obtained from the *Murex*, a mollusc on their coast, to the people of the Nile valley, and received in return many articles of Egyptian manufacture. Among the deposits of this time in the Palace of Knossos was found the lower half of a diorite statue, in late Middle Kingdom style, probably dating from the earlier part of the 13th Dynasty.

Traders from Crete probably landed at Alexandria, for there have been found at the Pharos near that town remains of a harbour, now many feet below the present level of the sea. One of the breakwaters of this harbour is paved on the top with the 'mosaiko' pavement so characteristic of this period.

As has been hinted, a new trade had arisen with the West, though it did not reach large dimensions until the next period; there is, however, some evidence that Cretan traders were visiting Malta about this time. Cretan influence was paramount in the Cyclades, and it seems probable that these islands were governed by the merchant princes of Crete, who, however, may have been of Cycladic origin. There is little evidence for the presence of these islanders upon the mainland of Greece until somewhat later.

About 1700 B.C. a great catastrophe occurred, which brought the Second Middle Minoan period to an end. All the palaces and villas in central Crete were destroyed by fire. Meyer has suggested that this might have been the work of the Hyksos, or Shepherd Kings, who invaded Egypt about this time. Other authorities dismiss this suggestion for what appear to be adequate reasons. The Hyksos were nomads, accustomed to travelling rapidly by land but unaccustomed to the sea. Their arrival in Egypt was by successive raids of small bands, rather than by a well-organized invasion, and it seems impossible that they could have extended these raids for hundreds of miles across the sea to destroy a flourishing civilization. The most reasonable suggestion is that a rebellion took place in the island. Glotz has advanced the idea that the great prosperity of the island had been developed by merchant princes of Cycladic or Anatolian origin, who had made themselves masters of the aboriginal population and those that had arrived in early days from Libya. Their rule had been too harsh, and this led to a revolution in which the palaces and houses of the masters had been burned to the ground.

FIG. 40. A Cretan shrine: restored by Sir Arthur Evans.

Whatever the cause of the disaster there seems to have been a dynastic change. The palaces were almost immediately restored and remodelled, with tall columns, tapering towards the base, and elaborate frescoes on the walls. At Knossos there was a shrine for the worship of a goddess depicted holding a snake in either hand, with an altar upon which rested a number of painted shells of *Pectunculus*, behind which was an equal-armed cross of marble. In another hall was a great ceremonial double-axe, evidently an object of worship, belonging to a cult which is believed to have been of Carian origin. It is evident that the new monarchs were of the same Cycladic or Anatolian type as their predecessors, though Hall has suggested that this change of dynasty indicates the destruction of the Carian thalassocracy, or maritime supremacy, by Minos.

With the dawn of the Third Middle Minoan period Crete entered upon its golden age. Large villas, like that at Hagia Triada, arose in various places. and the eastern half of the island, which had been depressed since the Early Minoan period, now recovered some of its former prosperity. The hieroglyphic writing was succeeded by a linear script, which was far more convenient; and to the close of this period we must ascribe the famous Phaestos disk, with its spirally arranged hieroglyphs, which is certainly a foreign importation, and is thought to have come from Lycia.

During this last stage the 'egg-shell' pottery finally disappeared and the polychrome ware was going out of fashion; towards its close naturalistic designs began to reappear. Vases also occur with shell inlay, which suggest Babylonian influence. The art of cutting stone vases revived, but the finest work was still carried out in the precious metals. A cup, from a tomb in the island of Mochlos, recalls in shape the famous gold cups discovered at Vapheio on the mainland, to which we shall return later.

The Aegean in the Early Bronze Age 89

Bronze spear-heads now came into use, at first provided with broad tangs, which were bent round the shaft to form a socket. Later the sockets were cast at the outset; thus the socket was

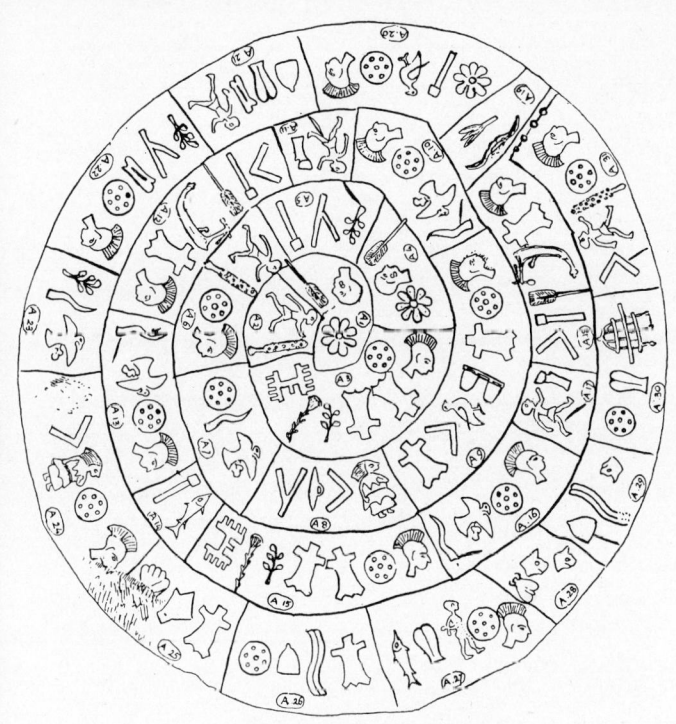

FIG. 41. The Phaestos disk.

independently invented in two distinct regions and by two distinct methods. Flat axes gave way to double axes, which, however, occurred, though rarely, as early as the Second Early Minoan period. To this time belongs a very interesting ivory draught-board, found in the Palace of Knossos.

Trade with Egypt was at a standstill during this century,

owing to the rule of the barbarous Hyksos in that land. Towards its close, however, relations were again resumed, since in the palace was found the lid of an *alabastron* bearing the name of Khian, a Hyksos king who reigned in Egypt about 1650 B.C.

Debarred from the south the Cretan merchants turned to the north and effected settlements on the mainland of Greece. Among the first cities to be founded by them were those of Tiryns and Mycenae, both in the plain of Argolis, the former near the coast, overlooking the sea, the latter near the head of the plain, where the trade-route to the Gulf of Corinth enters the mountains. Both had been the seats of early Cycladic invaders, but with the arrival of these Cretan merchants the type of their civilization was completely changed. The wealth of these cities, even at this date, vied with that of Knossos and Phaestos, and the gold objects of this time found in these cities, and elsewhere on the mainland, surpass anything yet found in Crete. The finest and best known of these are the famous repoussé gold cups found in a tomb at Vapheio, the workmanship of which has not been equalled in any metal work that the ancient world has yet produced. In some of the shaft-graves at Mycenae, which may date from this time, were found long rapiers of bronze.

The spread of Cretan trade at this time to the head of the Gulf of Corinth was doubtless due to the fall of the Second City of Hissarlik, the trade from which had formerly passed this way. This resulted in the expansion of Cretan trade to the West, where its presence can be traced by the occurrence of segmented beads of glass. Segmented beads of stone occur in Crete as early as the Second Early Minoan period, but in glass they are of later date. Such beads occur in Egypt from the 11th to the 19th Dynasties—that is to say, between 2200 and 1210 B.C.; in Crete from the beginning of the Third Middle Minoan to the end of the Third Late Minoan periods, from 1700 to 1200 B.C. Bone beads of this type occur among the Early Bronze Age deposits in Malta and at El Argar in south-east Spain, while similar beads in glass have been found at Fuente Alamo in Spain, at

FIG. 42. Gold cup from Vapheio.

sites in Brittany, in Dorset and Wiltshire in England, and in Ayrshire in Scotland.

About 1600 or 1580 B.C. the Palace of Knossos was again destroyed by fire. This time the destruction was due neither to an invasion nor a rebellion but was caused by an earthquake. Evans has suggested that this was connected with the volcanic eruption that occurred in the island of Thera about this time; that eruption, however, seems to have taken place somewhat later, as fragments of Late Minoan pottery were found beneath the lava. The destruction of the palace brought to an end the

Middle Minoan period about the time that the Hyksos were expelled from Egypt.

We have seen that during the period under discussion in this chapter Cretan influences extended throughout the Cycladic islands; and it seems probable that they were under Cretan government. During the Second Middle Cycladic period the

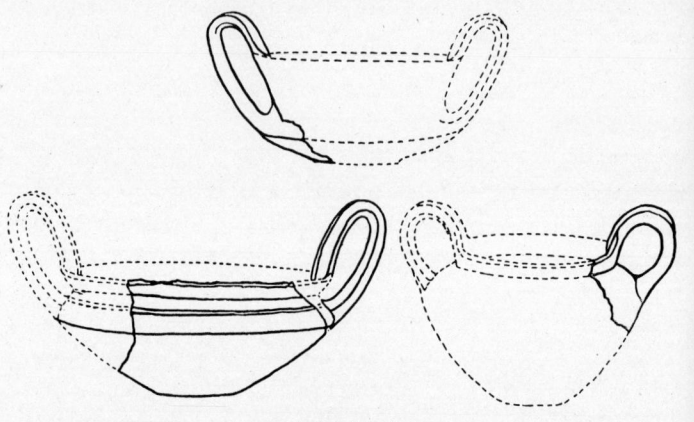

FIG. 43. High-handled vases.

city of Phylakopi was enclosed within strong fortifications, which makes us suspect that the Cretan overlords were afraid of attacks from some other quarter. This seems likely, since influences, other than Cretan, are apparent in the tombs of this date in the islands of Euboea, Naxos, and Syros.

We must now turn to the mainland. We have seen, in previous volumes, that about 2300 B.C. civilization in Thessaly entered its Third period, which lasted until about 1800 B.C. It was during this period that a fresh type of pottery appeared in the Valley of the Spercheios, which empties into the Maliac Gulf near the northern end of the island of Euboea. The arrival of a fresh type of pottery suggests the coming of a new people, and it becomes important to form an opinion as to the affinities of these new-comers.

This new culture possessed cups with high handles, sometimes fantastically elaborated, jugs with cut-away necks, perforated stone axe-heads and mace-heads. Pottery of these types has been found over a wide area, stretching from the Dardanelles to the Adriatic, and its association with perforated stone axe-heads or battle-axes has suggested that it betokens the arrival of people under leaders from the border of the steppe using an Indo-European tongue. On their arrival in the Spercheios valley these people settled at first around the head of the Maliac Gulf, between Thessaly and Phocis; and since not far away, in the south of Thessaly, there was once a territory known as Hellas, it has been thought that these new-comers were the first Hellenes, the people responsible for the earliest Hellenic dialects, the Aeolic, Ionian, and Cypro-Arcadian.

It is possible, however, that still earlier intruders into Thessaly, those who introduced the Dhimini ware about 2600 B.C., were under similar leadership, and were responsible for one of these dialects, but this is a question for the moment incapable of proof. If this were so, it seems likely that these earlier invaders introduced the Aeolic dialect.

It seems probable that it was some of these Hellenic invaders who destroyed the Second City of Orchomenos about 1900 B.C., and were responsible for the Third City that arose upon its ruins. If so, it seems likely that they were the makers or users of the so-called Minyan ware that was found there in such quantities. The fact that the city was destroyed, perhaps by the Hellenes, about the same time that the Second City of Hissarlik fell before an attack of a similar type suggests that there may be some distant connexion between these two events.

The Third City of Orchomenos was twice rebuilt, and the Hellenes seem to have extended their rule rapidly in a southerly direction, for Minyan pottery has been found generally distributed from Thessaly in the north to Argolis in the south. It occurs also, as has been already hinted, in tombs in Euboea, Naxos, and Syros, and has been reported from the island of Levkas in the west and from Macedonia still farther north. It would seem, then, that these Hellenes not only overran nearly all the mainland that was afterwards Greek but made considerable advances into the islands. This domination of the Hellenes, with their Minyan ware, lasted from 1900 to about 1625 B.C.

About 1650 B.C. the Second City at Lianokladi was destroyed and a Third City arose on its site, but about 1625 B.C. Minoan influence, mentioned above, was felt in the Peloponnese, and before long the merchant princes of Crete had become dominant throughout the greater part of Greece, and the Hellenic rule came for a time to an end. Meanwhile over the greater part of Thessaly, which about 1800 B.C. entered its fourth phase, the state of civilization was very backward and the pottery coarse, plain, very roughly made, and badly baked.

While we must leave the discussion of the site of Hissarlik and the Mycenaean civilization of Greece to be dealt with in the next chapter, a word must be said here on the earlier remains found at Tiryns, Mycenae, and other early Greek sites. The earliest houses at Tiryns are rectangular with apsidal or semicircular ends. This is a northern type and seems to have been brought from Thessaly. Though the Cretans probably arrived here about 1625 B.C., no marked change is noticeable until the beginning of the Late Minoan Period.

Mycenae was a Helladic settlement of long standing, but a powerful Cretan prince seems to have established himself there about 1625 B.C. It is thought that members of this family were interred in the second, fourth, and fifth of the shaft-graves found here by Schliemann, with rich accompaniments, including, in two cases, golden masks covering the faces of the deceased. The mask from the fourth grave shows the face of a beardless man, but that in the fifth grave has a beard, a feature unknown to the Cretans, and suggesting that the occupant was of another

FIG. 44. Gold mask from first shaft-grave at Mycenae.

race. There are many difficulties in interpreting the evidence from these shaft-graves, but the discussion of this must be left to the next chapter. In several of these graves fragments of amber were discovered, suggesting that the lords of Mycenae traded with the Baltic, through the Adriatic and the Gulf of Corinth.

It is somewhat doubtful, in spite of certain traditions,

whether the Cretans at this time had established colonies at Corinth, Orchomenos, or Thebes, though there is no doubt that their influence had spread to these places, as well as throughout the Peloponnese, to the northern shore of the Gulf of Corinth, and to Ophrys on the Saronic Gulf.

BOOKS
BAIKIE, JAMES. *The Sea Kings of Crete* (London, 1910).
BURROWS, RONALD M. *The Discoveries in Crete* (London, 1907).
CHILDE, V. GORDON. *The Aryans* (London, 1926).
EVANS, A. *The Palace of Minos at Knossos, Crete* (London, 1921 and 1928).
GLOTZ, G. *The Aegean Civilization* (London, 1925).
HAWES, C. H. and H. B. *Crete the Forerunner of Greece* (London, 1909).
MYRES, J. L. *Who were the Greeks?* (Berkeley, 1930).

8

Crete and Mycenaean Greece

AFTER the destruction of the palaces and villas by the earthquake, which occurred about 1590 B.C., Crete entered its First Late Minoan period. The palaces and villas were rebuilt, but Knossos seems now to have become the capital of the island, while Phaestos, though still important, played a secondary part. Many other flourishing towns now arose in the island, some of which had existed, though of little consequence, during earlier periods. The most important of these were Tylissos, Mallia, Gournia, Pseira, Palaikastro, and Zakro. These were well laid out, with narrow paved streets, and contained houses of various sizes to suit the needs of different types of people. The larger mansions, like the palaces, were built round courtyards, and in nearly all cases had bathrooms.

The palaces were reconstructed on the old model. They contained suites of private apartments, large halls for administrative

Fig. 45. The Cup-bearer fresco.

purposes, workshops, and long ranges of storerooms, and were fitted with a very efficient sanitary system. The walls were decorated with frescoes, the finest examples of which have been found in the Villa at Hagia Triada, though that of the Cup-bearer, from the Palace of Knossos, is perhaps the best known.

The pottery is elegant in shape, and many of the vases are of great size. The fabric was not, however, so good as in earlier times, for the clay was often badly refined while the pots were insufficiently baked. The decoration was of bold naturalistic design in dark paint on a light ground, but towards the close of the period the designs became more conventional. The rarity of small cups and jugs of fine pottery suggests that these were still often made of metal, and for some purposes stone was used also. To this period belongs the famous Harvesters vase, beautifully carved out of black steatite, in light relief, and representing a band of harvesters with their tools merrily returning from work. Other well-known vases, from this time, or perhaps a little earlier, are known as the Gladiator and the Chieftain vases.

The numerous frescoes that adorn the walls, as well as the engraved seal-stones, give us a good idea of the costumes of the period. The men were clad in a simple loin-cloth and a short kilt; these were drawn in tightly at the waist, producing a wasp-like effect on the figure. Into the loin-cloth was sometimes thrust a short dagger. The ladies wore long and elaborately flounced skirts, tight at the waist and wide at the ankles; their bodices were low in front, exposing the breasts, while behind the necks they rose like Medici collars. Both sexes wore bracelets on their wrists, to which were attached engraved seal-stones.

The linear script, introduced during the previous period, continued in use, and the earlier hieroglyphs had completely disappeared. The crouched burials, covered by jars, continued as before. The art of the sculptor reached a high pitch at this time,

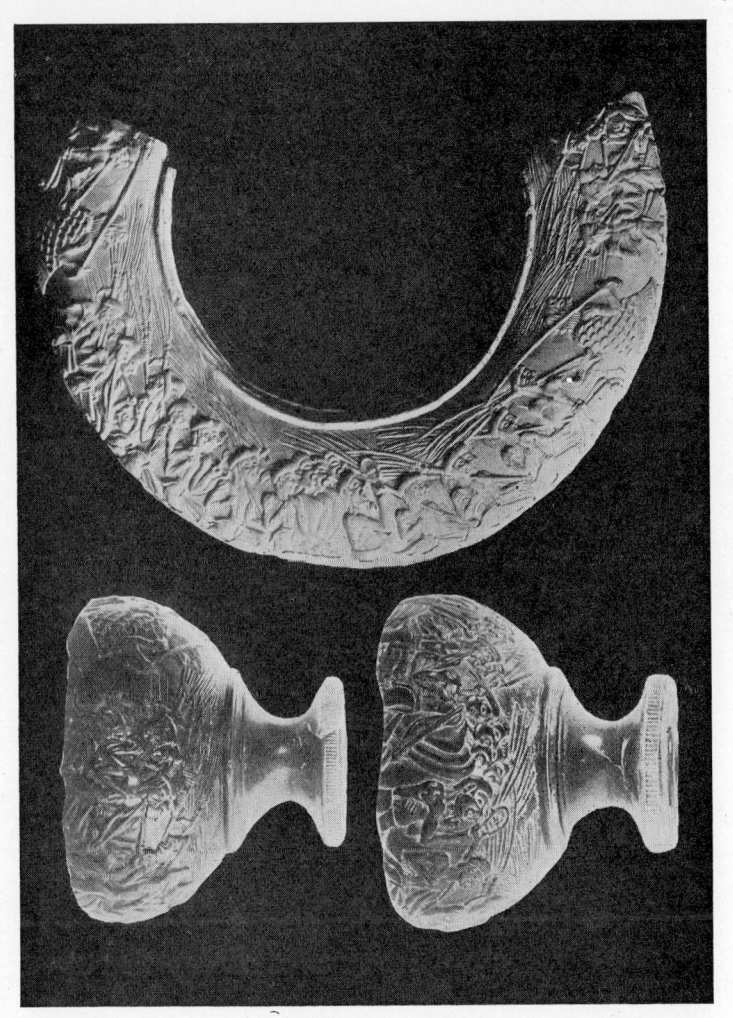

FIG. 46. The Harvesters vase.

the chief material used being ivory, sometimes combined with gold. The best-known works of this type are the ivory and gold figure of the snake goddess and the figures of the boy leapers.

FIG. 47. Ivory figures of boy leapers.

During this period the majority of the Cyclades remained dependent upon Crete and were ruled by the merchant prince of Knossos; this is especially true of the islands of Melos and Thera. Trade was resumed with Egypt, now that the Hyksos had been banished and the land had again come under the rule of native kings. In the tomb of Rekmere, an important official of Thutmes III, which dates from about 1440 B.C., is a fresco depicting men of Keftiu bearing gifts in vases that are clearly of Cretan make and belong to this period. There is some difference of opinion as to whether these Keftians were Cretans or not, and it has been suggested that they were inhabitants of the southern coast of Asia Minor. Hall believed that they were Cretans, though he admitted that this term might have been used to include the people from the neighbouring Asiatic coast. There is no doubt, however, that the things that they are represented as carrying were of Cretan origin. Though a close intercourse was carried on with Egypt, relatively few objects of Egyptian origin have been found in the Cretan deposits of this date. One can only suppose that, as the Cretans carried wine and oil to Egypt, they received in exchange other equally perishable commodities.

About 1450 B.C. the civilization of Crete is considered to have entered its Second Late Minoan period. This, however, applies only to Knossos, where a particular type of pottery was in fashion, somewhat similar to that of the preceding period but more florid and elaborate in its decoration; this is known as the Palace style. The rulers of Knossos seem to have become more powerful and to have been supreme over Crete and the neighbouring islands. To this period belongs the throne room, with its carved stone throne, and to this date we may perhaps attribute the story of Minos, the law-giver.

About this time we find jar-burial giving way to tombs cut in the rock; these were of two kinds—plain shaft-graves, like those found in an earlier period at Mycenae, and cave-like tombs opening out of pits. Both types of tomb have been found in the cemetery of Zafer Papoura. In some of these were long bronze rapiers and socketed spear-heads as well as Egyptian scarabs dating from the close of the 18th Dynasty, and, most important of all, some beads of Baltic amber. In a tomb at Isopata, near Knossos, were found a series of alabaster vases of Egyptian origin. At this time a new form of linear script came into use.

About 1400 B.C. the Second Late Minoan period came to an end when the Palace of Knossos, all the other palaces and villas and the towns as well, were burned down. The cause of this catastrophe is uncertain. Some have suspected a rebellion, like that which took place some centuries earlier, while others believe that the destruction was caused by a foreign invader. The majority tend to the latter view and suggest that the invaders came from the Peloponnese; this seems likely, but whether it was the subject merchant princes of the mainland, who revolted against the dynasty of Minos, their supreme lord, or whether the cities in the Peloponnese had passed into the hands of Hellenic conquerors, must be left for discussion later. The legend of Theseus and the Minotaur suggests that the invaders came from the shores of the Saronic Gulf, perhaps from Athens, more probably from Troezen, where the cult of Theseus was first established.

The catastrophe that overtook Knossos and the cities of Crete not only brought to an end the Second Late Minoan period, but it also terminated Cretan supremacy, seriously damaged Cretan trade, and brought the glorious days of this island civilization to an end. Thenceforward the centre of interest lies on the mainland of Greece, to which we must now turn our attention.

A small fortified citadel was built at Tiryns during the early part of the Late Minoan period, but the majority of the buildings now to be seen on that site, including the massive casemates with false arches, which have aroused the wonder and admiration of visitors since the days of Classical Greece, belong to a later date, after the final catastrophe at Knossos.

At Mycenae, too, we have no very certain remains of this period, though some believe that a small citadel existed here on the top of the acropolis. Our information as to the civilization of this period comes from the contents of the graves, especially

FIG. 48. The throne of Minos.

from those known as the shaft-graves. As we saw in the last chapter, some of these seem to date from the closing years of the Middle Minoan period, but the majority go back no further than the earliest phase of the Late Minoan. The gold masks that cover the faces of the deceased have already been mentioned, and some of these, notably that from the fifth grave, represent bearded men with broad faces. Since all the men shown on the Cretan frescoes and on the engraved seal-stones have long and narrow faces, and are always clean-shaven, the presence of these bearded masks has led some to suspect that a new element was present in the population of Mycenae, and was represented among its ruling caste. This may be so, but the evidence is not quite clear as yet. What this alien element was is almost equally obscure, though we may suspect that it was Hellenic in origin, since Minyan ware had been widely distributed over this area before the arrival of the Cretans.

With these gold masks were found many gold diadems, breast-plates, bracelets, and seals, as well as many cups of gold and silver. Among the weapons were fine bronze daggers, inlaid with precious metals, the designs representing hunting scenes. Besides these there was a number of beads, mostly of amethyst from Egypt, but many of amber, which must have come from the Baltic. The pottery from graves was, for the most part, of typical Late Minoan style, with naturalistic decoration but of poor technique.

Certain details in the history of Mycenae are subject to dispute. Evans, for instance, believes that the well-known carving of two lions rampant, one on either side of a pillar that surmounts the gateway leading into the upper town, dates from the beginning of this time, while Wace and Hall believe that it was erected after the final catastrophe at Knossos. Again, Evans believes, though here again some differ from him, that most of the *tholoi* or domed tombs date from the First Late

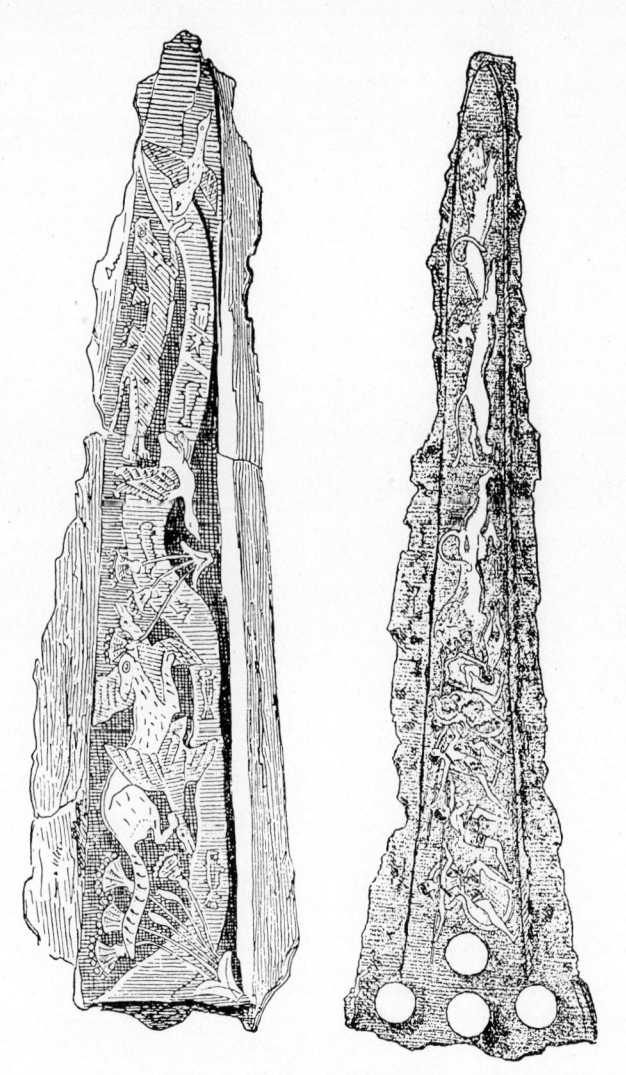

FIG. 49. Mycenaean daggers.

Minoan period, some going back, perhaps, to still earlier times. The best known of these *tholoi* is that known as the Treasury of Atreus, parts of the pillars from the entrance of which are in the British Museum. Since all these tombs have been found rifled, it is not easy to determine their dates with precision, but Hall suggested that the Treasury of Aegisthus dates from the first half of the First Late Minoan period, that those at Pylos, Triphylia, the Messenian Pylos, and Vapheio date from the second half of the same period, while Evans believes that the Treasury of Clytemnestra dates from the closing phase of the Third Middle Minoan period—that is to say, between 1625 and 1580 B.C. Evans is also of the opinion that all these *tholoi* are earlier than the shaft-graves. We have seen, however, that the contents of some of these graves must date from the close of the Middle Minoan period. To get over this difficulty, Evans has suggested that the bodies in the shaft-graves, together with the goods accompanying them, had originally been buried in the *tholoi*, but had been removed and reinterred in the shaft-graves at a later date, when times became unsettled, because the shaft-graves lay within the fortifications while the *tholoi* lay without.

Mycenae seems to have been the centre from which all the Cretan settlements on the mainland were governed, and from which radiated Cretan influences almost to the confines of Greece. Its chief satellite towns were Tiryns, Corinth, and other settlements in the Peloponnese, such as the two towns named Pylos; but it traded with the north, being connected with Thebes and other centres of Boeotia through Thisbe, while its commerce reached as far as the south of Thessaly. Its position at the head of the plain of Argolis, lying astride of the road which here entered the mountains on its way to the north, enabled it to control all the trade which came from the Gulf of Corinth towards Tiryns and Nauplia to be carried thence across the sea to Crete. Its main wealth lay in gold and amber. The latter had doubtless been carried from the Baltic overland through the Elbe Gap to Linz on the Danube, or through the Moravian Gate to the neighbourhood of Vienna, and thence round the eastern foot of the Alpine range to Fiume on the head of the

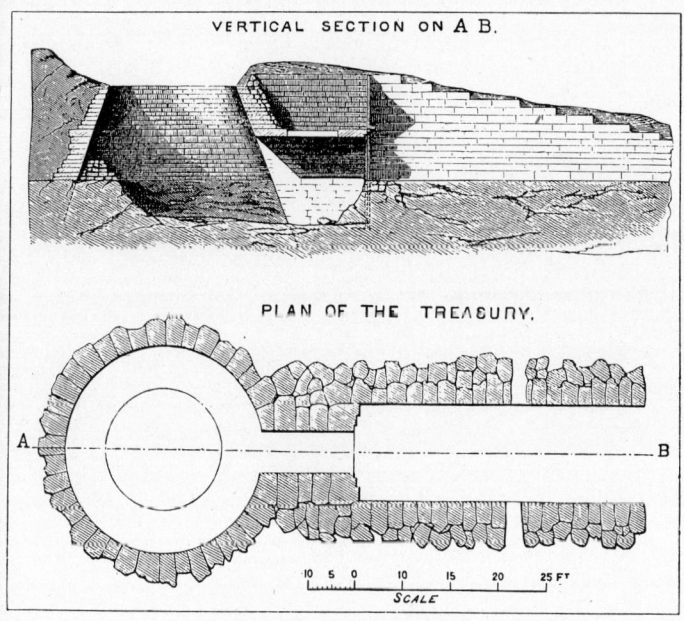

FIG. 50. The treasury of Atreus.

Adriatic, whence the sea route to the head of the Gulf of Corinth was easy. Where the gold came from is not so clear. It may have come by a similar route from Transylvania, where, as we saw in an earlier volume, gold was mined at a very early date, or it may have come from one of the western goldfields, from Spain, Portugal, Brittany, or even from Ireland.

About 1500 B.C. it is thought that a new dynasty arose at Mycenae, and some think that the *tholoi* were the work of the new rulers. This, however, seems unlikely. It seems to us more likely that, as *tholoi* had been in use in Crete since Early Minoan days, though they were going out of fashion during the latter part of Middle Minoan times, it was the new-comers from Crete about 1625 B.C. who introduced the custom into the Peloponnese, where it had been unknown before. We are inclined to suspect that the new dynasty may have been Hellenic, the former makers of the Minyan pottery, who must have formed a considerable element in the population of Mycenae during the period of Cretan domination. It may well be that some of the subject people overthrew their rulers and set themselves in their place. This would not have effected any marked change in the civilization, since the mixed population of the city would have remained much as before.

The shaft-graves still present difficulties. Some of their contents clearly go back to the earliest period of Cretan domination, yet the form of the graves was unknown in Crete before this, though a few somewhat like them occur at Zafer Papoura rather later. Moreover, one of the occupants of these graves wore a beard, a practice unknown at that time in Crete. Besides this the form of the shaft-graves might well have been developed from the pit graves formerly used by the makers of the Minyan ware.

On the whole, in spite of the early date of some of their contents, we are inclined to place the shaft-graves later than the *tholoi*, and as being the burial custom of the new dynasty, which we suspect was Hellenic. It may be that the last king of the 1st Dynasty fortified the city, already threatened by the Hellenes, and removed the bodies of his ancestors with their grave furniture to a safer place; more probably the new kings dug graves after their own fashion, and furnished the deceased monarchs with grave furniture robbed from the *tholoi* of their predecessors.

Crete and Mycenaean Greece

While this new dynasty was ruling in Mycenae an important city had arisen at Thebes, with a palace on the citadel, known as the Kadmeia. This may signify the arrival of a fresh group of merchants from Crete, as described in the story of Cadmus. The Fourth City of Orchomenos arose about the same time, and its inhabitants drained Lake Copais, thereby vastly extending the land suitable for cultivation. The Cretans about the same time crossed the Gulf of Corinth, landed on the plain of Crissa, and founded the oracle at Delphi, where their snake

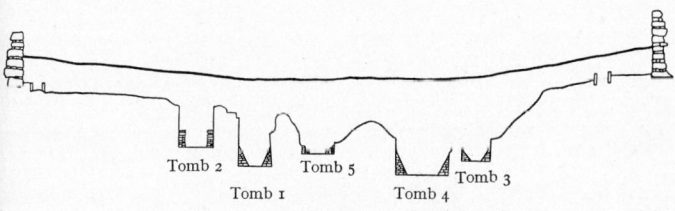

FIG. 51. Shaft-graves at Mycenae.

goddess was worshipped and the priestess or Pythoness gave out oracles. Mycenaean influence was also felt in Euboea, and tombs containing pottery of this age have been found at Chalcis.

Thessaly meanwhile was still in its fourth period, and was developing on its own lines, for it seems to have been completely cut off from the rest of Greece. Towards the close of the period Mycenaean pottery spread as far as its southern shores, around the Pagasaic Gulf.

No great break occurred in Greece comparable with the overthrow of the Cretan cities and palaces, and it would seem that those are likely to be right who suspect that the destroyers set out from the Peloponnese. If the suggestion that we have made is correct, that the Hellenic subjects of the Minoan lords of Knossos overthrew their masters about 1500 B.C. and usurped their power, we may suspect that it was the same Hellenes who, a century later, attacked the central seat of that power and destroyed its civilization for ever.

We cannot close this chapter without a few words on Hissarlik. As we saw in our last volume, the Second City of Hissarlik was sacked and burned about 1900 B.C. On its ruins there arose in time a humble village of poor huts known as Hissarlik III, and this again was succeeded by another village of shepherds, living in similarly simple style, which is called Hissarlik IV. Still later, at a date which cannot yet be fixed, but probably not far from 1700 B.C., a further settlement was made on the same site, the Fifth City, or Hissarlik V.

Though this settlement also consisted of simple and humble dwellings they were surrounded by a strong fortification, built of squared blocks of stone. This enclosed an area much larger than that occupied by the Second City, and was, in fact, the basis for the strong walls of Hissarlik VI. Everything points to the fact that this city was erected by a people newly come to the district, for though some of the pottery was of the plain monochrome type, with occasional incised ornament that had been used since the site was first occupied, much of it shows shapes and designs quite new to the locality. There were vases, painted in coloured slip with a free hand, often with naturalistic designs, usually depicting plants. The occasional presence of the spiral has been thought to denote connexions with Crete and the Aegean Islands, but may well be related

FIG. 52. Pottery from Hissarlik V.

to the spirals that occur at Butmir and throughout the Danube basin.

It is clear that with the Fifth City a new and important chapter opened. Dr. Leaf saw in this the basis of the story of the building of the city for Laomedon by Herakles. This may be so, but it seems more likely that we may see in the new-comers who founded the city the arrival of the Dardanians, who probably arrived in Asia Minor about this time from the Balkan peninsula, in which there were two regions, in Illyria and north Macedonia, known later as Dardania. It is probable that, like the Hellenes, they had leaders from the steppe-borders and spoke an Indo-European tongue. If our views are correct, then the Fifth City of Hissarlik was founded by a wandering tribe from Macedon, not altogether unrelated to that Hellenic group that came down the Spercheios valley into south Thessaly and probably worshipping the same series of deities.

The Fifth City of Hissarlik gave place to the Sixth, the Troy of Homeric legend. When it was founded is uncertain, for most of the remains found belong to a late stage of its existence. If some of the pottery found in it is really Minyan, as has been claimed, its origin must go back almost, if not quite, to 1650 B.C., for this ware seems to have ceased in Greece soon after the arrival of the Cretan merchants in the Peloponnese, about 1625 B.C. On the other hand, it is stated that the earliest fragments of pottery found in this city are late examples of the First Late Minoan period, and it is claimed that the Minyan ware is not truly so, but a late type of Helladic matt-painted ware that is descended from the true Minyan. Among the early wares found were also geometric wares from Lianokladi and white wares from Cyprus, which are similarly of Late Minoan date. If these wares really date from the first occupation of this city, then its foundation cannot be placed much earlier than 1500 B.C. Myres, however, believes that it arose not earlier than 1400 B.C.

It is impossible as yet to decide these points, though doubtless fresh light will be thrown upon the problem when more progress has been made in the decipherment of the large number of Hittite tablets that have been brought to Europe and are being studied by Hrozny, Forrer, and other scholars. The full account of the Sixth City, Priam's Troy, must be left to our next volume, when we shall deal with its fortunes and tragic end.

BOOKS

BAIKIE, JAMES. *The Sea Kings of Crete* (London, 1910).
BURROWS, RONALD M. *The Discoveries in Crete* (London, 1907).
CHILDE, V. GORDON. *The Aryans* (London, 1926).
EVANS, A. *The Palace of Minos at Knossos, Crete* (London, 1921 and 1928).
GLOTZ, G. *The Aegean Civilization* (London, 1925).
HAWES, C. H. and H. B. *Crete the Forerunner of Greece* (London, 1909).
MYRES, J. L. *Who were the Greeks?* (Berkeley, 1930).
SCHLIEMANN, H. *Mycenae* (London, 1878).
SCHLIEMANN, H. *Tiryns* (London, 1886).
SCHLIEMANN, H. *Ilios* (London, 1880).
SCHLIEMANN, H. *Troja* (London, 1884).

9

Trouble in the Near East

THE centuries between 1900 and 1600 B.C. witnessed widespread disturbances, especially in the old kingdoms of the Near East. These were overrun by tribes from the steppes and deserts, and this gives some support to the view that this period was a dry one as suggested in Chapter 5, a period when steppe and desert dwellers had overflowed into the settled areas on their borders. On this occasion the violence of these raids may have been due to the fact that the steppe peoples, and after them the desert tribes, had recently domesticated the horse, thus enabling them to acquire greater mobility for their forces.

In chapter 10 of *The Way of the Sea* we described the ruin that fell upon Babylon, owing to a raid by the Hittites in 1870 B.C., which brought its 1st Dynasty to an end. After that, for more than a century, anarchy prevailed in Mesopotamia, though the kings of the Sea Country maintained a semblance of order near the Persian Gulf until about 1703 B.C., and the Assyrian monarchy remained intact until about the same time. The intervening area was a prey to marauders from the north, the desert tribes from the south, and the mountaineers from the Zagros range. At length, at a date usually given as 1746 B.C., but which Sydney Smith suggests should be considered as about 1740 B.C., Gandash, a Kassite chief, seized Babylon, and founded the Second Babylonian or Kassite Dynasty.

Since the Kassites became the ruling power in Mesopotamia for a period reckoned by tradition as 576 years and 9 months we must try to learn their type and affinities. The people of the Zagros range were a hardy group of mountaineers who had troubled the settled folk of the plain since the earliest times. Their affinities are uncertain. They may have been a south-eastern group of that eastern Alpine or Armenoid type which provided most of the population of Asia Minor, in which case they probably spoke an Asianic language. Or they may have been allied to the Elamites and kindred tribes living farther to the south-east, in which case their language would have been more akin to some still spoken in a few of the valleys of the Caucasus.

We have seen that as early as the time of Sargon, if not before, there had been people in the foothills of the Zagros range, the peoples of Su and Gu, or the Subaraean tribes, that seem to have been, in part at least, those folk from the northern steppe who have figured so largely in *The Steppe and the Sown* and *The Way of the Sea*. These we believe to have been of Nordic type and using an Indo-European speech. Such people seem to have formed the ruling caste among the Kharrians and Hittites, and, since the names of the Kassite kings have a very Indo-European appearance, we may suspect that these hardy mountaineers had come under Nordic leadership before they established their rule in Mesopotamia. It is usually believed that the Kassites introduced the horse and the chariot into Mesopotamia. This may well be so, though this animal is first mentioned in the time of Hammurabi. In fig. 16 in *The Steppe and the Sown* we showed an earthenware figure of a mounted man, dug up in 1925 at Kish in a cemetery, which was then believed to have been abandoned before 2700 B.C. We pointed out then that the animal there portrayed might have been an ass rather than a horse, but we have since learned from the excavator of this cemetery that the graves were far from being as old as was at first thought, and were those of Parthians dating from the early centuries of the Christian era. We may conclude, then, that though the horse was known in the time of Hammurabi, when it was called the 'ass from the east', it was the Kassites who brought it and the chariot into general use in Mesopotamia.

Gandash, the first Kassite king of Babylon, had only a small dominion, perhaps only the capital, but later he added Nippur to his domain. We know little of his acts, but that he restored temples at both cities; he died about 1730 B.C., when his lands passed to his son Agum I, who ruled them till his death about 1709 B.C. Whether he died childless or was slain by a rival chief is uncertain, but he was succeeded by Kashtiliash, son of Burna-Buriash, who was a contemporary of Ea-gamil, the last king of the Sea Country. About 1703 B.C. Ula-Buriash, a brother of Kashtiliash, acting as his general, conquered the Sea Country, thus extending the Kassite dominions to the shores of the Persian Gulf, and about the same time further conquests were made to the north-west, up the valley of the Euphrates.

Kashtiliash died about 1687 B.C., and for a time our knowledge

FIG. 53. Kudurru, or boundary stone, of the Kassite period.

of events in Mesopotamia is a blank. The royal lists tell us of thirty-six kings; the names of thirty-five of these are known, but their monuments and inscriptions are so scarce that it is impossible to draw up a connected account. Nothing of moment is known until the time of Agum II, who was reigning about 1561 B.C.

The Kassites, like all steppe folk, were illiterate, and though they employed Sumerian scribes to record their actions, the records became fewer and less full as time went on. Almost the only monuments for a great part of the period during which they ruled are a series of boundary stones, which usually cannot be dated with precision, and which tell us nothing of the history of the country. Mesopotamia was passing through a Dark Age.

Of the Hittites and Kharrians we know little more. In *The Way of the Sea* we traced the story of the Hittites to the time of Telibinus, who died about 1800 B.C., when he was succeeded by his son Mursilis II. On his accession Mursilis confirmed the actions of his father, making one of his brothers, Malik-Arakh, governor of Carchemish, and another, Rimi-Malek, ruler of Aleppo. Then he started on an expedition against Harran, probably held by the Kharrians. No record has been found to tell us of the fate of this expedition, and for a time the history of the Hittites is a blank. It probably consisted mainly of constant feuds with the Kharrians and other warlike tribes under Nordic rule, but, like Mesopotamia, the Hittite and Kharrian regions enter a Dark Age until the appearance of Dudkhalis, king of the former, about 1450 B.C.

We saw in our last volume that the 12th Dynasty of Egypt came to an end in 1788 B.C., and that during the succeeding 13th Dynasty the land was not prosperous and the monuments few. This lack of prosperity seems to have been due to an invasion of a nomadic steppe folk from Asia. It has usually been thought that these arrived a century later, but information recently obtained by Sir Flinders Petrie from his excavations in Palestine has led him to believe that these tribes entered the eastern part of the delta during the closing years of the rule of the 12th Dynasty, and that it was their appearance and the disorganization of trade that followed their arrival that brought the 12th Dynasty to an end. It would appear that these nomads arrived in a series of small waves of invasion, till at length they had taken possession of the eastern half of the Delta, where they set up a dynasty, known to later historians as the 15th. Meanwhile the rest of the land was governed, not very successfully, by the 13th Dynasty, whose acts we have described in *The Way of the Sea*. On the fall of this dynasty, about 1690 B.C., the invaders subdued the greater part of the land, leaving a number of petty native princes ruling in various provinces. Those with their capital at Thebes claimed to be the 14th Dynasty; among these were three kings known as Intef III, IV, and V. At length the invaders, known as the Hyksos or Shepherd Kings, set up one of their number as chief ruler over the whole land, and he ascended the throne as the first monarch of the 16th Dynasty.

The origin of the Shepherd Kings is wrapt in mystery. They arrived in Egypt from Palestine, where they continued, as we shall see, to have settlements after their arrival in the Delta. Most writers to-day believe that they came from north Syria, and that they were some of those Semitic tribes who had given much trouble to the descendants of Sargon, and one of which had established the 1st Dynasty of Babylon. It is believed that the advent of the Kassites in Mesopotamia and the advance of the Hittites and Kharrians into north Syria had so disturbed the people of that region that some migrated southwards into Palestine and then crossed the peninsula of Sinai to settle in Egypt. This seems a plausible explanation, but we must remember that these Shepherd Kings were the first to introduce into Egypt the use of the horse and the chariot, and these were first used by the Kassites, Kharrians, and Hittites, people believed to have had rulers of Nordic type, derived ultimately from the northern steppe. It is just possible that these invaders of Egypt, made up largely of people from north Syria of Semitic speech, and joined by nomads from Palestine and Transjordania, may, like the other peoples who disturbed the peace of the world at this time, have had leaders of Nordic type with Indo-European speech.

On their arrival the Shepherd Kings fixed their seat of government at Avaris, the site of the later Pelusium, a city which stood at the mouth of what was once the most eastern branch of the Nile. This site lies somewhere near the coast a few miles east of Port Said. Another important city of theirs is believed to be represented by the mound, called Tell el-Yehudiyeh, or 'the mound of the Jewess', near Zagazig in the Delta, while a third city was called Sharuhen. At the beginning of the 16th Dynasty they settled at Memphis, the old capital just south of Cairo, and ruled the country from there.

Though they were occupying the greater part of Egypt, they still retained a hold on their former possessions. A great earthwork, surrounded by a trench eighty feet wide and twenty-eight feet deep, with a raised fort in the centre, has recently been explored by Sir Flinders Petrie at Beth-pelet in south Palestine. Here he found a number of tombs of the subjects of the Shepherd Kings, containing skeletons lying stretched at full length, great water-jars, daggers and toggle-pins, as well as scarabs which showed that these tombs dated from after their arrival in Egypt.

Little is known of the history of the country during the early days of their rule, for the Dark Age had enveloped Egypt as well as the other countries in the Near East. Manetho, the historian of Egypt, records the names of several of their kings, but it is difficult to identify them with monarchs that have left us any inscriptions. It is not until the closing phase of the period that any light is given to us by contemporary monuments, and such light as has been vouchsafed is meagre.

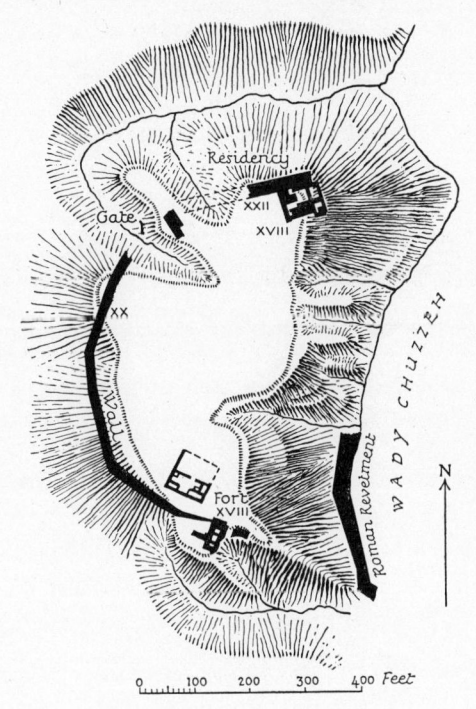

FIG. 54. Earthwork at Beth-pelet.

It may be taken as certain that it was during this Dark Age that the Hebrews, traditionally led by the aged Jacob, came, on the invitation of Joseph, to start their long sojourn in Egypt, where they were granted territory in the land of Goshen. Josephus, indeed, is prepared to argue that the Shepherd Kings themselves were Hebrews, a view to which Hall was half prepared to agree. Josephus was, however, bent on the aggrandizement of the Jewish people, and anxious to attribute to them such a magnificent achievement as the conquest of Egypt. As we have seen, it is likely that, when the north Syrian tribes moved southwards on their journey of conquest, other tribes in Palestine and Transjordania would have joined them to share the spoils. Some Hebrews, who in their wanderings from Ur had passed first to Harran and thence to the south of Palestine, might very well have joined the conquering horde. From the account handed down to us in the Book of Genesis it seems more likely that they arrived a generation later, and settled among kindred tribes that had formed part of the original expedition.

It will be remembered that Joseph obtained his release from prison and his high position as the Chief Vizier of Egypt by prophesying that, after a period of abundance, there would be a number of lean years. We are also told that it was during one of these lean years when, owing to scanty rainfall, their crops had failed, that Jacob learned that there was corn in Egypt and sent his sons to purchase supplies, and eventually moved into the country with his tribe. Ellsworth Huntington has endeavoured to show that a slight reduction in rainfall, which might be only of trivial inconvenience in many lands, might so affect the vegetation of the steppes as to make them uninhabitable both for man and beast. Such slight desiccations have occurred, he thinks, from time to time during the course of human history, and at such times the steppe men become restive and endeavour, usually successfully, to invade the cultivated lands on their border.

The previous pages have shown that soon after 1900 B.C. there was evidence of such unsettled conditions as there had been about 2700 B.C., and that by 1800 B.C. these had become acute. We shall see, too, that about 1600 B.C. circumstances had again changed and that settled government reappeared in Egypt soon afterwards, when conditions improved elsewhere in the Near

East. While the spread of the tamed horse through some steppe folk may have been the immediate cause of these raids, as we

FIG. 55. Fragment of a sitting statue of Khian.

suggested in *The Way of the Sea*, the story of Joseph warns us that the theory of occasional droughts as important factors cannot wholly be ignored.

There have been recovered from inscriptions the names of a few of the Shepherd Kings, mostly dating from the close of the period of their domination; three of these, at least, have Semitic names. There were several named Apopi, and after Apopi I came Khian, of whom we have several inscriptions, including one on

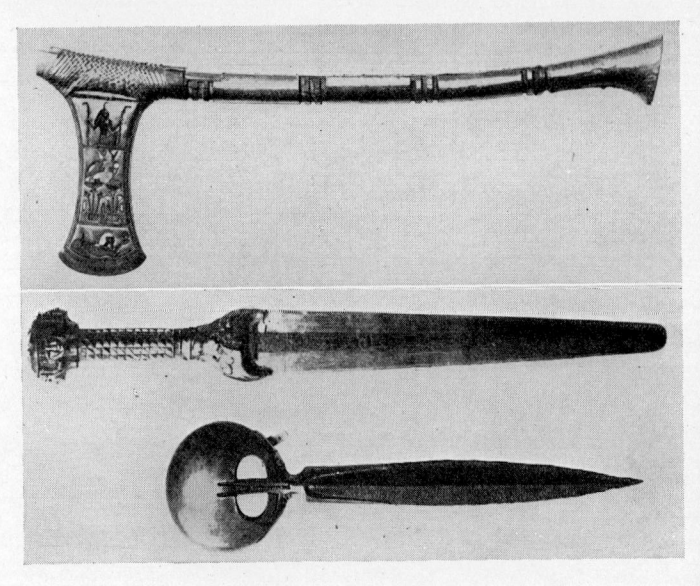

FIG. 56. Bronze weapons of Ahmose I.

the lid of an *alabastron* found in the Palace of Knossos. He was succeeded by Apopi II, who reigned for thirty-three years, and later by Apopi III, in whose time a war broke out between the Shepherd Kings and the rulers of Thebes, to whom we must now return.

About 1620 B.C. Sekenenre I was reigning at Thebes; he was a king of the 17th Dynasty, who ruled a small province in the south. He began a war of liberation, and before his death he had driven back the Shepherd Kings from the district of Thebes. He was succeeded about 1615 B.C. by Sekenenre II, who carried on the movement, wresting still further portions of the land from the invaders. In 1605 B.C. he was succeeded by Sekenenre III, who married a Royal Egyptian Princess, Aah-hotep, by whom he had three sons, Kamose, Senekhtenre, and Ahmose. Sekenenre III was killed about 1590 B.C., though whether he was assassinated or fell wounded by the invaders is uncertain. His three sons came to the throne in succession, each apparently driving the invader still farther to the north and east. Ahmose, the youngest, ascended the throne in 1580 B.C., proclaimed himself first king of the 18th Dynasty, and two years later took the capital city of Avaris, and in 1575 B.C. the city of Sharuhen, thus bringing the rule of the Shepherd Kings in Egypt to an end.

BOOKS
BREASTED, J. H. *A History of Egypt* (New York, 1912).
DELAPORTE, L. *Mesopotamia* (London, 1925).
Cambridge Ancient History, vol. i (Cambridge, 1923).
HALL, H. R. *The Ancient History of the Near East* (London, 1920).
SMITH, SIDNEY. *Early History of Assyria* (London, 1928).

10
Iranians, Aryans, and Chinese

IN the last three volumes of this series we have often referred to the nomads roaming the steppes of south Russia and Turkistan, and in *The Steppe and the Sown* we described how some of these, having tamed the horse, spread out in various directions to conquer the peasant populations beyond their borders. Some, however, remained behind, and the fortunes of these must engage our attention in this chapter. We have given reasons for believing that these steppe folk were of that robust and long-headed type usually called Nordic, although perhaps they were not quite so generally fair-haired and blue-eyed as some of their descendants who settled in the Baltic region at a later date. We have also expressed our opinion that it was among these people that there developed the ancestral forms of that group of languages known as Aryan or Indo-European.

The surest evidence of the existence of a people is the material remains that they have left behind them—pottery, tools, and dwellings; these tell us of their existence, and enable us to picture their manner of life. In the case of the remnant of the steppe folk, which had not left the grass-lands in the third millennium B.C., we have no such remains to help us. This is partly because the eastern end of the steppe has not yet received much attention from the archaeologist, but more because the steppe folk, being of nomadic habit, had few material possessions, and these mostly of a perishable nature, while their frequent change of abode prevented an accumulation of remains in one spot. Though archaeological material is lacking, we have some evidence which points to the presence of such people at the eastern end of the steppe at the time with which this volume is concerned.

In the last pages of chapter 9 in *Peasants and Potters* we described the Aryan hypothesis, and pointed out that during the closing years of the eighteenth century this theory was first put forward, and that during the three first quarters of the nineteenth comparative philologists were busy working out the connexions between the majority of the European tongues and a few of those spoken in Asia, and searching for what was called the Aryan cradle. For a long time such studies were concentrated on the Vedas, the earliest books of the Hindu Brahmans, and the religious books of the Parsis, who were found to be the descendants of the ancient Persians. These books will be described later, but the important point that emerged from the study of these two literatures was that the earliest volumes were nearly contemporary, and that the languages in which they were written were so nearly alike that the people could not long have been separated when they were composed. A similar resemblance was noted in the religious views and practices as well as the deities in both series.

Although the resemblances were considerable there were marked differences, and these also are instructive. Thus the *devas*, or good spirits of the Rig-veda, become the *daêvas* or demons of the Avesta, the *Asuras* or evil spirits of the Sanskrit books are the Ahuras or good spirits of the Iranian texts, while the sacred *Soma* of the Hindus, the liquid that drops from the Cosmic Tree of Life, is known to the Parsis as *Haôma*, the juice of a certain plant, which is pressed out by them on the altar with much ceremony. The higher castes of the Hindus call themselves *Aryas*, or nobles, while in the Avesta the supreme deity is made to say: 'The first of the good lands and countries I created was the *Airyana-Vaeja*'—that is to say, the 'Aryan Home'. These are only a few samples of the resemblances between the two languages, but they will suffice. The chief difference is that where the Aryans of India use an *s* the Iranians use an *h*, a difference that exists between Latin and Greek. There is also a resemblance between the religious ideas of both peoples, who have left us many hymns in honour of their deities, but here the difference is more profound. The Aryans worshipped a number of gods—Dyaus, the sky, and Varuna, like the Greek Ouranos, also the sky, and often associated with Mitra, 'the Friend', to mean daylight. Then there was Agni, the sacred fire, and Indra, the storm god. The Iranians were strict monotheists, with a

FIG. 57. Mortar, pestle, and strainer for Haôma.

dualist theory, believing in a supreme deity, Ahura-Mazda, the god of light and good, for ever warring with Ahriman, the power of darkness and evil.

It is clear from these close resemblances in their tongues and religion that these two peoples formed at one time a single group, occupying a definite region, and it has been thought that it was the difference that arose in their religious views that caused them to separate into two parts, which ultimately occupied very distant lands. Various traces of a former polytheism in the Iranian books show us that this form was the older, and so it has been thought that a prophet arose who preached a monotheistic religion, to which half of the Aryans were converted, and that this change led them to separate from those who continued to cling to the older customs. The close resemblance between the language used in both sets of books shows us that this separation could not have occurred many centuries before they were composed, and since the *Rig-veda* was compiled, as we shall see, not later than 1200 B.C., it is believed that this separation must have taken place about 1500 B.C. It may, however, in our opinion have occurred a century or two earlier.

In A.D. 641 the Arabs defeated the Persians at the battle of Nehavend, near Ecbatana, and brought the whole country under Muslim rule. The conquerors compelled all the inhabitants to conform to the faith of Islam, and they persecuted those who adhered to the old religion. A number of these fled to the East, and at length found refuge in the peninsula of Gujarât on the north-west coast of India. Here they remained until about A.D. 1300, when they were driven forth again by a Muslim invasion of that district. They took refuge in Nâvsâri and Surât, and later in Bombay, where they are to-day the prosperous community of the Parsis.

It was early realized in Europe that the Parsis had sacred books, but their contents were unknown. At the beginning of the eighteenth century George Bouchier, while visiting Surât, obtained from some Parsi priests a manuscript which he gave to the Bodleian Library at Oxford. Here it remained for long unknown and unread. Tracings of four of its pages reached Paris, where they were seen by a young scholar, Anquetil Duperron. Keen to learn their meaning, he joined the troops of the French East India Company, and sailed with them for the East in A.D. 1754. He was absent seven years, during which he had learned as much of the language in which this manuscript was written as he could from the Parsi priests. He returned in A.D. 1762, and in 1771 published a work in three quarto volumes entitled *Zend Avesta, the work of Zoroaster*. This work was not well received by the learned world and, as it turned out, the translation was in many ways very inaccurate; still it was the first version of one of the sacred books of the Parsis to appear in a European tongue. Later on, more accurate translations were made, and the language in which they were written was found to be an early form of ancient Persian, and was for a time called *Zend*, after the title of the most important of these books, which was known as the Zend-Avesta. Afterwards it was found that this title was more correctly read *Avesta-u-Zend* ('The Law and the Commentary'), and the work is now known as the *Avesta*, and the language in which it is written is called Avestan.

The *Avesta* is in four parts, none of which is quite complete, as many copies perished when Persepolis was destroyed by fire during its occupation by Alexander the Great in 331 B.C. It is said that the works survived only in the memories of the priests until the Sassanian monarchs, who ruled Persia from A.D. 226 to 641, convoked a council of priests to restore the text and to commit it to writing. The four remaining parts of the *Avesta* are: the Yasma, containing the Gathas or hymns; the Vispered, or doxologies; the Vendidad, or law book; and the Yashts, or hymns to angels. Of these the Gathas are said to be the oldest.

The *Avesta* is said to have been the work of Zarathustra, better known in the West as Zoroaster. He was a prophet, and certainly reformed the religion; it has been thought that he was responsible for the monotheistic reforms that are believed to have caused the separation of the two branches of the Aryan people. It is possible, however, that this separation occurred before his time. Much depends upon the date at which he lived; on this there have been various conjectures, ranging between 6000 and about 660 B.C. One authority states that he was born in 600 B.C. and died in 583 B.C., but there is much to be said for the view that the *Avesta* is nearly contemporary with the *Rig-veda*, which, as we have seen, dates from about 1200 B.C. If Zarathustra lived at this time, which is likely, the reforms in the religion were carried out some centuries after the separation of the two groups. One thing is clear: Zarathustra was responsible for the strictly monotheistic form of the Iranian religion, for the three cardinal principles that he taught were:

1. Agriculture and cattle-breeding were the only noble callings.
2. The whole creation is a combat between good and evil.
3. The elements—air, water, fire, and earth—were pure and must not be defiled.

Little is known of the life of Zarathustra, but it is stated that he was a member of the Spitâma clan, a native of Azerbaijan, and was born at Urumya. Later in life he travelled eastwards and met Vistasp, known in later legend as Gushtasp, the chief of the Iranians, at Kishmar in Khorasan. At Vistasp's court he carried out his religious reforms, and during his stay there the Iranians were attacked several times by the neighbouring Turanian tribes, who are thought to have been of Mongol origin. During the second of these attacks Zarathustra met his death at Balkh.

The First Farjand of the Vendidad tells us of the early history

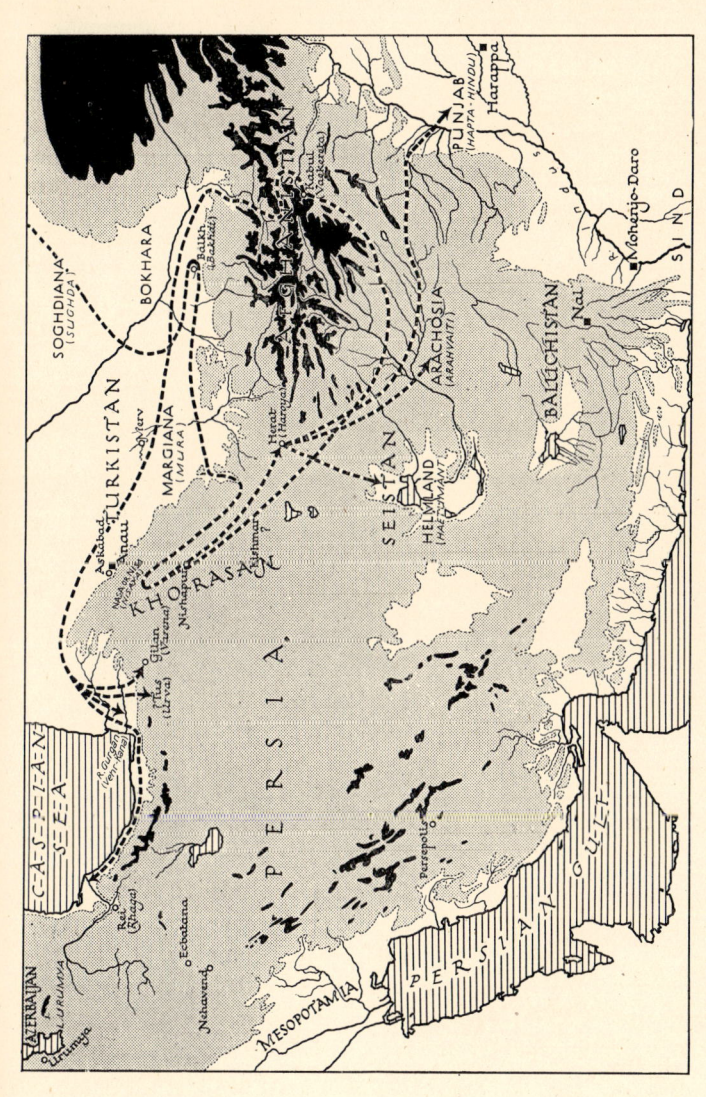

Fig. 58. Map showing the movements of the Aryans. Land above 10,000 ft. black; between 2,000 and 10,000 ft. stippled.

of the Iranians as it was believed in the time of Zarathustra. It is said that they, or the undivided Aryans, once lived some distance to the north, in a country known as *Aryanem-Vaejo*. Then the Power of Evil made this land icebound and uninhabitable, and the Aryans moved southwards to Sughda, or Soghdiana, and Mura, or Margiana, the country around Bokhara and Merv. A plague of locusts forced them to leave Sughda, when they were driven by hostile tribes to Bakhdi, the country of lofty banners, now the district around Balkh. From Bakhdi they moved on to Nisaya, which has been thought by some to have been Nishapur, but was more probably Nasa or Nisa, south of Askabad.

At this time, according to these legends, the group divided, one part going to *Haroyu*, the modern Herat, and the other to *Vaekereta*, the land of noxious shadows, believed to have been Kabul. These groups again divided, the first into tribes that occupied *Arahvaiti*, now Arachosia, *Haetumant*, now the Helmand, and *Hapta-Hindu*, or the Punjab. The group settled at Kabul divided into four tribes, settled respectively at *Urva*, the modern Tus, *Vehr-Kana*, the Gurgan, *Rhaga*, the Rei, and *Varena*, the Gilan.

If these legends are trustworthy, it was this second subdivision of the original Aryan group that led to the settlement of the Indo-Aryans in the Punjab at a date which cannot be later than 1400 B.C., and is probably earlier. If King Vistasp ruled at Balkh when the undivided Aryans occupied that district we must place the date of Zarathustra much earlier than we have done so far, but it seems more probable that this monarch's rule in that city must be placed later by some centuries.

Beyond the few statements already cited, the Avesta tells us little of the doings of the undivided Aryans or of the Iranian group during the centuries following their separation. Many legends of kings and heroes have been handed down, and these were combined together into a national epic, known as the *Shahnama*, by the poet Firdausi, born about A.D. 937. While many of these tales are mythical or unreliable legend, there is a substratum of truth in the later parts, though legendary and historical characters have been much confused. The story tells of constant wars between Iran and Turan, between the Iranians and the Mongolian tribes that bordered them on the north-east. The most famous describe the exploits of their great hero Rustem, and the tragic episode in which he slew his son Sohrab has been made familiar to English readers by Matthew Arnold.

The group that settled in the Punjab are called the Aryan invaders of India. They have a number of sacred books of great antiquity, handed down orally among the Brahmans, or priestly caste, and written down at a much later date. The most important of these are: the *Rig-veda*, the *Mantras*, the *Brahmanas*, and the *Sutras*. These are composed in different forms of the Sanskrit tongue, and are of different dates. Max Müller divided the Vedic period, during which these books were compiled, into four sub-periods, that of the *Sutra* literature 600–200 B.C., the *Brahmanas* 800–600 B.C., the *Mantras* and the later parts of the *Rig-veda* 1000–800 B.C., and the *Chandas*, the oldest hymns of the *Rig-veda*, 1200–1000 B.C. These dates are generally accepted.

The *Rig-veda*, the oldest of the series, is a collection of 1017 hymns, divided into ten books of unequal length. Books ii–vii, each composed or collected by a different priestly family, are the earliest, books i and viii are later, book ix is composed of a selection from the others, while book x is evidently more recent. These hymns contain many references to the rivers in the Punjab, and even to the Kabul river and one of its tributaries, but it is believed that when the earlier books were compiled the Aryans were living near the Sarasvati river, south of the town of Ambala. It is clear, however, from the allusions to the other rivers, that the Aryans had passed through the Punjab on their way from Afghanistan to the Sarasvati basin. That they had reached the latter district by 1200 B.C. seems clearly established, and we must, it would seem, postulate that their entry into the basin of the Indus occurred not later than 1400 B.C.

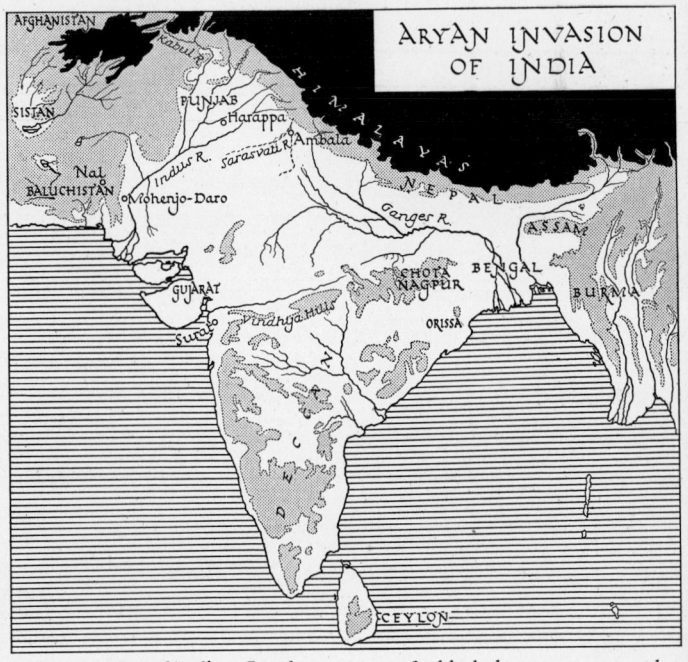

FIG. 59. Map of India. Land over 10,000 ft. black; between 2,000 and 10,000 ft. stippled.

We must consider the state of India and its population at the time of their arrival. The peoples of India to-day are mainly long-headed, but they vary considerably in other respects. Broad-headed populations occur on the north-west and north-east; these seem to be later intrusions. The peoples of Burma, many of the inhabitants of Assam, and those dwelling in Nepal and elsewhere on the foothills of the Himalayas are broad-headed with Mongoloid features, and the same type, in a modified form, is found throughout Bengal and Orissa. These appear to be relatively late intruders from the Tibetan plateau. On the north-west frontier many of the hill tribes are also broad-headed, though they show no resemblance to the Mongols. These seem to be relatively late arrivals, though the presence of certain broad-headed types farther south in the western and north-western parts of the peninsula suggests that they may have been slowly percolating the mass from a very early time.

The majority of the Indian population is, however, long-headed, and among these we must distinguish various types. In the north-west we find tall men of light complexion with brown wavy hair, very narrow straight noses, and heads which are extremely narrow, with a cephalic index often about seventy-two, accompanied by high foreheads. The ancient form of extreme narrow-headedness with forehead receding rapidly from prominent brow-ridges is absent here; we are dealing rather with a type that seems to have a mode of growth involving special development of the profile. In most of the rest of India, and especially in the Deccan, the general population is more moderately narrow-headed, with cephalic indices more in the neighbourhood of seventy-five. The noses are moderate, shorter, and somewhat broader than in those first described, the lips are fuller, the colour darker, the stature shorter, and the hair wavy to curly. Among the wilder peoples of the hills and jungles, especially in south India, Chota Nagpur, and Assam, the type changes again. One finds there men with very dark skin and wavy or curly hair. Their noses are very broad and their heads very narrow, often with an index about seventy-two, but their foreheads usually recede and their brows are often strong. These are the types that were found to resemble so closely the Badarian skulls from Egypt that we described in chapter 1 of *The Way of the Sea*.

The very dark broad-nosed and long-headed people are remnants of an early drift of population; the moderately long-headed folk of the Deccan, with noses moderate to broad, represent a subsequent drift, and the tall people with extremely narrow heads and strong profiles a still later one.

This interpretation of the racial make-up of the long-headed people of India is borne out by a study of their languages. In many parts the hill and jungle folk still talk languages belonging to the linguistic group known as Austric, which extends through Malaya and the East Indian Islands across the Pacific Ocean as far as Easter Island and across the Indian Ocean to Madagascar. Of these Austric languages the Munda tongues are spoken by various hill and jungle tribes in many parts of the peninsula.

South of the Vindhya Hills, and to some extent in Ceylon, we find Dravidian tongues, Tamil, Telegu, and Kanarese, while north of this, and among some aristocrats in the south, we find Aryan dialects. Though many speculations have been made on the subject, no satisfactory affinities have been found for the Dravidian tongues, but it is clear that they were once spoken in the north of the peninsula, especially in the north-west, for Dravidian characteristics have been noted in Vedic and Classical Sanskrit; besides this there is in the mountain region of Baluchistan a large area in which Brahui, a Dravidian dialect, is still spoken. In the Ganges valley and the Punjab the only tongues spoken are the Aryan dialects, till we come to the foothills of the mountains, and even there in the north-west such dialects prevail.

These facts seem best interpreted by supposing that the whole of India was first peopled by a small dark race with broad noses and wavy to curly hair, and small and very narrow heads, allied to the Badarians of Egypt and the Veddas of Ceylon, the Toalas of the Celebes, the Batu of Sumatra, and perhaps to the natives of Australia, and that these people used an ancestral form of the

FIG. 60. Various types of Indian people. *a*. Hill tribesman, Nilgiri Hills; *b*. Dravidian girl; *c*. Hindu fakir; *d*. Brahman lady.

Munda and various other languages of the Austric group. Then came another race, taller with less narrow heads, brown in colour, with noses of medium width and curly hair, somewhat resembling the brown race that inhabits north Africa to-day, a race which is usually considered as a southern variety of the Mediterranean race. These were, one is tempted to think, the people who introduced the Final Capsian culture, with its microlithic flint implements, into India and Ceylon. Analogy would suggest that this people introduced the Dravidian languages. On the other hand these tongues seem to bear no resemblances to the Hamitic dialects of north Africa, which are believed to be the present representatives of the languages spoken by the Final Capsians.

In earlier volumes we have made reference to the great discoveries made by Sir John Marshall at Mohenjo-daro and Harappa in the Indus valley. Here he found a high civilization, dating, he believes, more than a thousand years before the arrival of the Aryans in that district. The origin of this civilization is obscure. It can hardly have arisen independently among the Late Capsian invaders of the peninsula, for it seems to appear fully developed in the Indus basin. Some have suspected a Sumerian origin, others think the Sumerian civilization came from the Indus basin, and a more plausible suggestion is that both came from some site between the two. It is possible that it came from Turkistan and is related to the early culture at Anau; or more probably it is derived from that early culture, with painted pottery, recently discovered by Professor Herzfeld in Persia, which seems to be ancestral to the earliest wares at Susa. The last suggestion is the more likely, for painted pottery, very like that found at Mohenjo-daro, has been found at Nal in Baluchistan, while fragments of a painted ware have been brought back by Sir Aurel Stein from Sistan. Whatever be the affinities of these dwellers by the Indus, it seems more probable that they were a relatively small number of civilized people who absorbed a larger number of the primitive folk that they found occupying the country on their arrival, and that they were responsible for the Dravidian tongues. This receives support from the fact that a Dravidian dialect is still spoken in the mountains of Baluchistan, at no great distance from Nal. Be this as it may, it was this culture, and this mixture of peoples, talking Dravidian tongues, except in the outlying regions, that the Aryan invaders met with, and by degrees conquered, on their arrival in the Indus Basin. These were the people that the Aryans called Dasas or Dasyus.

We cannot close without a word on Chinese legend. In *The Way of the Sea* we described how T'ang, the Prince of Shang, overthrew the wicked emperor Chich Kwei in 1766 B.C., bringing to an end the Hsia Dynasty and founding that of Shang or Yin. T'ang, sometimes called Ch'öng-T'ang, was a man of noble mind, and is said to have been a descendant of Yu, the founder of the Hsia Dynasty. He was a firm and wise ruler, and is said to have been a great sportsman, being much addicted to hunting and fishing.

During the rule of this dynasty the empire was divided into feudatory states under great chiefs, who held almost independent power, though recognizing the supreme rule of the emperor. Chief among these was the Duke of Chou, whose land lay to the north-west, where it abutted on the deserts of Mongolia. This chief had to maintain a considerable army to keep off the Tartar hordes that were a constant menace to this part of the empire. The great nobles erected fine palaces, in which they lived in magnificent state, and governed in a patriarchal fashion.

The empire was considerably enlarged, down the Hoangho to the Pacific Ocean, northwards to the neighbourhood of Peking, and in the south beyond the Yangtse. The capital was moved on several occasions, generally owing to the floods of the

Hoangho. During most of the time the land prospered, fine bronze vessels are said to have been made, while inscriptions in archaic characters of this date, engraved on tortoise-shell, deer antlers and the clavicles of sheep, have lately been discovered at

FIG. 61. Early pottery of the Shang Dynasty. From the excavation at An-yang, in Honan province, conducted jointly by the Academia Sinica and the Freer Gallery of Art.

Hsiao Tun Tsun near Anyang in Honan. Musical instruments of various kinds were used, astronomy was studied to enable the calendar to be fixed, while much use was made of astrology and divination.

T'ang was succeeded in turn by twenty-seven descendants, of whom little is related, except of the last, Chou-sin, who ascended the throne in 1154 B.C. Early in his reign he attacked the State of Su, and brought back from that district a beautiful captive, the notorious Ta-ki, whom he introduced into his harem, and who exerted a most baleful effect upon his subsequent career.

Later Chinese writers have described her as shamelessly lustful and cruel, and have enlarged on her enormities, stating that the emperor became her willing slave. Sai-ma Ts'ien, who wrote a great history of China in the first century B.C., says of Chou-sin that 'he loved the pleasures of the cup and debauchery, and was

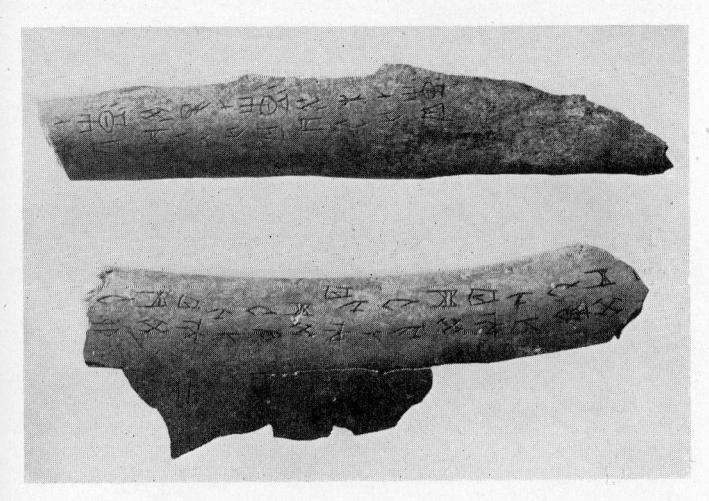

FIG. 62. Archaic inscription of the Shang Dynasty. From the excavation at An-yang, in Honan province, conducted jointly by the Academia Sinica and the Freer Gallery of Art.

infatuated with his consort, the beloved Ta-ki, whose words he obeyed'.

The ill-deeds of Chou-sin and of Ta-ki rapidly alienated the sympathies of his people, but for long they put up with his rule. The most prominent feudatory state was, as we have seen, the border province of Chou, at this time under the rule of Wön-wang. This duke had succeeded his father in 1182 B.C., and was recognized as a model of what a feudal prince should be. Two of his friends had made a fruitless attempt to cure the emperor of his infatuation for Ta-ki, for which effort they had been executed. Wön-wang expressed himself freely about the injustice of this deed, for which he was accused of *lèse-majesté* by the Marquis of Ch'ung. The popularity of the duke prevented the emperor from putting him to death, but he made him a prisoner at Yu-li in Honan. He was eventually liberated owing to the efforts of his son Fa, and returned to his duchy, which became a centre of disaffection. He died in 1135 B.C. at the age of ninety, when he was succeeded by his son Fa, who took the name of Wu-wang. Some years later, after careful preparation, Wu-wang raised the standard of revolt. In 1122 B.C. he attacked the forces of the emperor, who was utterly defeated, and took refuge in his palace, to which he had conveyed his most precious possessions. The fallen monarch then set fire to the building and perished in the flames. Thus ended the dynasty of Shang or Yin, and Wu-wang ascended the throne as the first monarch of the Chou Dynasty. It should be understood that Chinese history prior to the Chou dynasty is of the legendary type, but there seems to be some reason for thinking that, as usual, legendary history has a substratum of fact.

BOOKS
The Cambridge History of India, vol. i (Cambridge, 1922).
BENJAMIN, S. G. W. *Persia* (London, 1889).
SYKES, P. M. *History of Persia*, vol. i (London, 1915).
HIRTH, F. *Ancient History of China* (New York, 1908).

II
Recovery in the Near East

WITH the accession of the 18th Dynasty and the expulsion of the Hyksos the clouds lift from the history of Egypt, though for another century they obscure that of south-west Asia. Of the Kassite kings of Mesopotamia during this century we know little but the names, and these are derived mostly from outside sources. Agum II was reigning about 1561 B.C. and Kurigalsu I about 1536, while his son, Meli-shipak I, occupied the throne about 1511. Nazi-Maruttash I was king in 1486 B.C. and Burna-Buriash I in 1461, while Kurigalsu II, who is thought to have been a son of his predecessor, succeeded about 1435. He was followed, it is believed, by Kara-indash I, who was reigning in 1410 B.C., while Kadashman-Enlil I, whose sister married Amenhotep, king of Egypt, was on the throne in 1400. Burna-Buriash II, of whom we shall hear more later, was reigning as early as 1395 B.C.

The kings of Assyria, pressed by the Kassites on one side and the Kharrians on the other, contrived to retain their independence, though we know little but the succession of their monarchs. Enlil-nasir I succeeded Puzur-ashur III in 1586 B.C., and was succeeded by Nur-ili in 1561. He was followed in 1536 by Ishme-Dagan III, whose son Ashur-nirari I succeeded him in 1511, and was followed by his son Puzur-Ashur IV in 1480. Enlil-nazir II, believed to have been the son of his predecessor, succeeded in 1459 B.C., and was followed by his son Ashur-rabi I in 1440. Then followed in succession Ashur-nirari III in 1425, Ashur-bel-nisheshu in 1406, Ashur-rin-nisheshu, his brother, in 1398, Ashur-nadin-akhi in 1396, and Eriba-Adad, his son, in 1390.

Of the Hittites we are equally ignorant. Dudkhalis I was ruling them about 1550 B.C., Hattushil II about 1500, and Dudkhalis II about 1450. His son, Shubbiluliuma, was reigning in 1411 B.C., when the cloud is partially lifted by the Hittite tablets brought back from Boghaz Keui. Among the Kharrians, to whom constant reference has been made, there had arisen a kingdom, organized on a feudal basis, and known as that of the Mitanni. These kings and nobles are thought to have been steppe-landers with Indo-European speech; they certainly worshipped deities with names resembling those honoured by the Aryans of India. The first king of the Mitanni of whom we hear was Shaushshatar, who was reigning about 1450 B.C., and his son, Artatama, succeeded him about 1430 B.C., and was followed by his son Shuttarna in 1410. He is believed to have been succeeded first by his son Artashumana, and later by his brother Tushratta, who was reigning about 1399 B.C.

About Egypt we have much fuller information. In 1580 B.C. Ahmose began his reign as first monarch of the 18th Dynasty, driving out the Shepherd Kings within a few years of his accession, and inaugurating the third great period of Egyptian prosperity, known as the New Kingdom, or more usually as the Empire. Scarcely had Ahmose thrust the Hyksos beyond his boundaries than his kingdom was threatened from elsewhere. Nubians revolted under the leadership of their Egyptian lords, and the king had to hasten southwards to quell this rebellion. This he did successfully, but it was some time before he established peace throughout the land, for other chiefs, descendants of feudal nobles of the Middle Kingdom, who had established separate governments under Hyksos rule, continued to assert their independence. These were reduced to submission, some were deposed, and the remainder were commanded to live at Thebes and to be members of the court rather than local governors of provinces. Thus the king established his complete supremacy and governed the whole country with the aid of his large army and a very efficient civil service.

Though he left few monuments, Ahmose established his dynasty on a firm foundation, not unlike that of the Emperors of Rome. He died in 1557 B.C., at an early age, and was succeeded by his son Amenhotep I. The new monarch was not left long in peace, for troubles arose again in Nubia. Amenhotep quelled this fresh revolt, and had established his rule firmly as far south as the second cataract, the boundary of Egypt under the Middle

FIG. 63. Amarna letter, No. 296, containing list of the dowry of Tushratta's daughter. Staatliche Museen, Berlin.

Kingdom, when he was called to a similar task in the western Delta. During the Hyksos domination the Libyans from the desert had encroached upon the fertile lands, and here endeavoured to maintain their independence. The new king brought these under his rule, and then turned to the north-east where, it would seem, fresh threats had come from the recently expelled Shepherd Kings. He led an expedition into Asia, and penetrated north Syria, even reaching the Euphrates, which he claimed as the boundary of his empire.

Amenhotep died about 1540 or 1535 B.C. It is uncertain whether he left a son entitled to ascend the throne, but in any case he was succeeded by Thutmose I, the son of a woman of unknown origin. Thutmose had first to put down troubles in Nubia, which he left in the charge of a 'Governor of the South Countries', and then turned to consolidate his Asiatic Empire. He marched through Palestine and Syria, exacting tribute from the numerous small states into which that region was divided, until he came to the Euphrates, where that river most nearly approaches the Mediterranean Sea. Across the river at this point lay the kingdom of the Mitanni, who were threatening to cross his frontiers. He seems to have defeated them, and to have had no trouble with the Hittites, who had formerly held north Syria; he erected a boundary stone somewhere near Carchemish and returned to Egypt, satisfied that his Asiatic Empire was firmly established.

Thutmose returned to Egypt and spent the rest of his reign in restoring the prosperity of his land and in adding to its temples. He had married Ahmose, the representative of the old line of Theban princes, and it is thought that this marriage was his sole right to the throne. She died when Thutmose was an old man, and as all her children but one had died during her lifetime she left an only daughter, Makere-Hatshepsut, who had been proclaimed heir to the throne. The declining years of

Fig. 64. Northern colonnades of Hatshepsut's temple at Der el-Bahri.

Thutmose were full of troubles, mainly concerned with the succession, for the people were determined to recognize no one but the royal princess.

Thutmose died about 1514 B.C., and what followed is obscure. Some think Hatshepsut succeeded to the throne, but was dispossessed by Thutmose II, a feeble and diseased son of the old Pharaoh by another wife. His reign was brief and of little consequence, and he died about 1501 B.C., when Hatshepsut remained sole monarch, though her claims were contested by a third Thutmose, the son of an obscure woman named Isis, by one, it is uncertain which, of the earlier bearers of his name. Thutmose III had begun his career as a humble priest in the temple of Karnak, but soon won the support of his fellow priests. Soon after the death of Thutmose II he effected a dramatic *coup d'état*, which was completely successful, and he ascended the throne on 3 May 1501 B.C., or, according to some authorities, three years earlier. He lost no time in marrying Hatshepsut, and they ruled jointly over the empire, the queen being, apparently, the predominant partner.

Hatshepsut is one of the most striking characters in Egyptian history. She was a great builder, and erected a magnificent temple against the western cliffs at Thebes, rising in a series of three terraces from the plain to the level of an elevated court. She was a wise and inspiring leader, and, finding that foreign commerce had not recovered from the depression caused by the Hyksos domination, she organized overseas expeditions to inaugurate fresh lines of trade, to search for new commodities, and to open up fresh markets. In her ninth year she sent an expedition to the land of Punt to obtain the myrrh necessary for the incense of the temple's services. Five vessels descended the Nile and passed through the canal, made during the Middle Kingdom, which led from the eastern Delta through the Wadi Tumilat to the Red Sea, and thence to Punt, which lay somewhere along its shores or beyond. She also resumed the working of the copper mines in the Wadi Maghara near Sinai, which had been abandoned for more than a century.

The work of Hatshepsut had been mainly at home, building and restoring temples and encouraging trade both at home and abroad; it had been essentially peaceful. During her long reign, which lasted until about 1479 B.C., the Egyptian armies had not set foot in Asia, and the tribes there felt that it was possible to regain their freedom. It was early in 1479 B.C. that the king of Kadesh, who had been the leader of the small states in Syria and Palestine, stirred up the city-states in that region to revolt under his leadership. This suggestion was readily followed by most of them, though the states in south Palestine, realizing that they would be the first to receive the brunt of Egyptian retaliation, did so with much reluctance. On 19 April 1479 B.C. Thutmose III started from Tharu, the modern Kantara, with a large army to put down the revolt. In nine days he had reached Gaza, and by the evening of 10 May he was on the slopes of Mount Carmel. Meanwhile the Syrians had occupied the fortress of Megiddo, on the north slope of that range, which commanded the only available pass. Then took place the first of many battles that have been fought at this site, which has given rise to the term Armageddon. Thutmose was victorious and took much spoil and many prisoners, though the king of Kadesh was fortunate enough to make his escape. Thutmose then marched to the Lebanon, took many cities in that neighbourhood, and returned to Thebes by October, having re-established his rule firmly over his Asiatic possessions as far as the south of Lebanon. The king of Kadesh still remained unsubdued, and the next year Thutmose undertook another expedition, in which he passed through the conquered territory, exacting tribute and receiving homage. Even the king of Assyria, anxious to escape attack from so famous a conqueror, sent costly gifts of lapis lazuli and horses. On his return to Thebes the victor set to work to enlarge the great temple of Karnak. Each year saw another great expedition and fresh conquests, and in the sixth campaign Kadesh was taken. In his eighth campaign he took Aleppo, defeated the Mitanni and established his boundary on the opposite side of the Euphrates near Carchemish. On his return from this expedition he was met by Hittite envoys, bearing gifts of eight massive rings of silver, some precious stones, and rare wood.

Expeditions to Syria to collect tribute, to inspire awe, and to punish rebel cities were almost annual events for the rest of Thutmose's reign, but he erected temples, which he endowed with a large share of his spoils. He enlarged his dominions to the south as far as the 3rd cataract and drew much precious metal from the Nubian gold mines. Feeling his strength failing him in 1448 B.C. he associated with him on the throne Amenhotep, his son by Hatshepsut-Meretre, a queen whose origin is unknown, and died in the spring of 1447 B.C., after a reign of nearly fifty-four years.

The exploits of Thutmose as a conqueror are quite without precedent. From early days kings of cities or small states had established their rule over other states of allied peoples, and had sometimes, as in the case of Elam, held for a time other small states in thrall; raiding expeditions, like that of the Hittites against Babylon, had taken place, while the conquest of settled countries, like Egypt and Mesopotamia, by desert tribes like the Hyksos, the Amurru and the Kassites, had occurred more than once. Organized expeditions, however, with large armies of soldiers, both on foot and in horse-drawn chariots, to conquer a number of alien states, had not been undertaken before the time of Thutmose III, with the solitary exception of the single venture of Thutmose I. In this the third Thutmose set an example, which was followed at intervals by such generals as Alexander, some of the Roman emperors, the Saracen leaders,

Jenghis Khan, Selim, and Napoleon, to mention only a few of the more conspicuous examples, and Thutmose III may claim the credit, if credit it be, of being the first to indulge in imperial expansion.

The death of the conqueror was the signal for revolt among the cities of Syria, and in his second year, 1447 B.C., Amenhotep led his army into Asia to put down the rebellion. This he did with ease, defeating the Mitanni barons near the Euphrates, and, having set up a boundary stone beyond that of his predecessor, he returned in triumph to Memphis, driving over 500 of the Syrian lords and bringing four-fifths of a ton of gold and nearly fifty tons of copper. Next year he undertook a similar expedition into Nubia for a like purpose, and placed his frontier station at Napata, just below the 4th cataract, thus bringing the whole of the fertile province of Dongola under Egyptian rule. After that he had peace for the remainder of his reign, which lasted for about twenty-seven years. He died about 1420 B.C., when he was succeeded by his son Thutmose IV.

This Thutmose was a younger son, and as a youth had no expectation of ascending the throne. It is related that as a young man he was hunting near the pyramids and slept at noon beneath the Sphinx, who appeared to him in a dream, announcing that he would in time become king, and praying that, when that happened, he would sweep his shrine free from the accumulated sand. When the prophecy was fulfilled, Thutmose piously undertook the task and set up an inscription to record the incident.

On his accession he had to lead an expedition through his Asiatic domains to establish order and to quiet the Mitanni barons. This he achieved, but, while in north Syria, he learned of a revival in the power and aggressive intentions of the Hittites, and thought it well to purchase a more definite alliance with the Mitannian people. He selected for this purpose Artatama, the principal Mitannian chief, and asked for his daughter in marriage. After some hesitation Artatama agreed to the proposal. Thutmose married his daughter, who took the Egyptian name of Mutemuya and became the mother of his successor. This is the beginning of the diplomatic, as distinct from warlike, relations that became such a feature of the next reign. After a brief campaign in Nubia in his eighth year, Thutmose IV died about 1411 B.C., and was succeeded by Amenhotep III, his son by his Mitannian queen.

Except for one expedition to Nubia, the reign of Amenhotep was peaceful and prosperous. The alliance with the Mitanni had produced the desired result, and diplomatic means were more successful than military expeditions for insuring peace with the subject peoples in Asia. These seem to have remained content with Egyptian rule, and to have vied with Mitannian chiefs, the kings of Assyria and Babylon, and the people of Cyprus in trying to gain the approval of the Egyptian monarch. Amenhotep was most friendly with his uncle Shuttarna, who had succeeded Artatama as king of the Mitanni, and in the tenth year of his reign married Gilukhipa, his uncle's daughter, who arrived in Egypt attended by a retinue of 317 ladies and servants. After the death of Shuttarna, his son Tushratta continued to adhere to the alliance, and sent his daughter, Tadukhipa, to be the bride of the prince, who subsequently ascended the throne as Amenhotep IV.

We have noted that the use of the horse, enabling people to traverse distances across the wilderness, previously only crossed with difficulty, brought the peoples of the Near East much closer together than had before been possible. One of the results of this was that the cuneiform script, long used in Mesopotamia, became the recognized writing for international correspondence, and with this, very frequently, went the Babylonian tongue. We have seen that from an early date there had been Mesopotamian traders settled in certain centres in Asia Minor. These, originally Sumerian, were by now accustomed to use the Babylonian language, and doubtless provided a staff of skilled scribes or secretaries to write the diplomatic correspondence for all the kings, chiefs, and governors in the Near East. The Egyptians, Mitanni, Hittites, and the people of Syria were all using this script and language for international correspondence at this time, and some of them adopted the script for their own languages. It is true that the king of Egypt and the Kassite kings of Babylon wrote always in Babylonian, but the Hittites wrote this language side by side with their own, which has resulted in enabling scholars to learn several of the Hittite dialects.

FIG. 65. A Tell el-Amarna tablet.

A mass of correspondence dating from this time has been found at Tell el-Amarna, the site of the city and palace founded by the next Egyptian king, while many more documents and letters of the same date have been recovered from Boghaz Keui on the Halys river in Asia Minor, the site of the Hittite capital. The tablets from these sites often refer to the same event, so that we have a complete series of diplomatic documents, enabling us to follow the international politics of this period.

It was a time of peace among the nations so recently at war, and of great prosperity in Egypt, which was still the dominant power. Babylon was relatively poor, while the alliance with the Mitanni enabled the Egyptians to keep in check the aggressive tendencies of the Hittites. Amenhotep III reigned long. He celebrated a jubilee in the thirtieth year of his reign and a third jubilee in his thirty-sixth year. About this time, however, all was not well in the north, for the Hittites had invaded Mitannian territory, though they had been repulsed by Tushratta. The Hittites were more successful in north Syria, and returned with booty from a raid on Katna in the Orontes valley. About the same time Aziru and his father Abd-Ashirta, chiefs of the Amurru, who had never willingly accepted the overlordship of Egypt, plundered the same region and the land around Damascus. Amenhotep was too old or too indolent to quell these revolts in person, but dispatched an army for the purpose; these troops restored order for a time, though the Hittites remained in possession of some of the southern lands of the Mitanni. Moreover the Habiru, nomad tribes from the desert, in whom we may possibly recognize the Hebrews under the leadership of Joshua, invaded Syria and Palestine, and it was during these troubles, about 1375 B.C., that the old king died.

Amenhotep III was succeeded by his son Amenhotep IV, a unique personality and the most interesting character in ancient history. He was the son of the late king by Tiy, a lady of striking character though of unknown origin, and was brought up by his mother and a priest named Eye or Aye. At an early age he married the beautiful Nefer-tete, who is thought to have been a princess of Asiatic origin. As neither the new king nor his father was descended from a royal princess of Egypt, it is believed by some that they were not looked upon as legitimate kings by orthodox Egyptians.

Amenhotep IV was an idealist but no man of affairs. He was

religious, sensitive, and a poet, and the hymns and psalms that he wrote will stand comparison with the best products of the Hebrew psalmists. He found his subjects worshipping many

FIG. 66. Ikhn-aton worshipping Aton.

gods with gross superstition and dominated by autocratic priests, the most powerful of which were those of Ammon, the deity of Thebes. He started a new religion, free from these baleful influences, on strictly monotheistic lines, calling his new conception of the deity the 'Aton', a name which had come into use for the sun during his father's reign; this was represented as a disk, from which emanated a number of rays, each terminating in a hand.

This new religion, though it received the sullen acquiescence of the majority of his subjects, roused the wrath of the priests, especially of those of Ammon. The king became unpopular in Thebes, his capital and the seat of the worship of Ammon, so he decided to found a new capital elsewhere. He selected a site on the right bank of the Nile halfway between Memphis and Thebes, and here he built a new city, which he called Akhetaton, the 'Horizon of Aton', where he erected a palace, in which he dwelt with his wife and daughters, his mother, and the priest Aye. The remains of this palace were found under a mound, known as Tell el-Amarna; here were discovered those tablets, containing the foreign correspondence of his father, which we have mentioned. At the same time he took a new name, Ikhnaton or Akht-aton, which means 'Aton is satisfied' or 'He in whom Aton is satisfied'.

We cannot give here a full account of the religion of Aton, the first monotheistic religion to appear in the ancient world, nor can we describe the reign of Ikhn-aton, or give an adequate estimate of this wonderful character. The subject forms the theme of many chapters in every history of Egypt and of special volumes describing the king and his times. It has been suggested that the idea of the new religion came from Asia, and was probably of Mitannian origin. This is possible. Several Mitannian princesses had married members of the Egyptian royal family about this time, and the Mitannians were related to those Iranians who had placed the sun in a leading position among their deities, and, under the influence of Zarathustra, eventually raised the concept into that of Ahura-Mazda, the God of Light, the supreme power of good for ever at war with the powers of evil and darkness, ranged under the banner of Ahriman. On the other hand the king was much under the influence of Tiy the queen-mother and of Aye the priest, both of whom were fervent adherents of the new religion and may well have been its originators; and we have no reason for believing that either was of foreign extraction. For the moment we must leave the origin of the reform unexplained and be content to note that during this reign a valiant, albeit unsuccessful, attempt was made to implant a monotheistic religion in the heart of the most polytheistic centre of the ancient world.

Under priestly influence painting had hitherto been formal and conventional, being restricted in its scope by religious traditions. At the palace of Amarna the decorations were free from this priestly restraint and blossomed out into a new and very naturalistic phase, quite unlike the formal paintings that were customary in the times preceding and following this period.

The absorption of the monarch in his reforms and religious exercises left him little time to attend to the demands of his empire, already showing signs of disruption at his accession. Though the Mitanni and Babylon remained for awhile on friendly terms, the Hittites lost no time in increasing their empire at the expense of Syria and the lands of the Mitanni. Tushratta, the king of the latter, remained faithful until he was slain by one of his sons and civil war followed; finally, Shubbiluliuma, the Hittite king, gave his daughter in marriage to Mattiuaza, the son and slayer of Tushratta, and forced the Mitanni to accept his sovereignty. Thus the Mitanni became ranged with the enemies of Egypt.

We cannot follow the details of the subsequent troubles; revolt follows revolt in rapid succession till it is difficult to make out their sequence, and at the time of his death, about 1358 B.C., in the seventeenth year of his reign, Ikhn-aton had lost all his foreign possessions, and the empire founded by Thutmose had come to an end. He was succeeded by Sakere, who had married his elder daughter Merit-aton, 'Beloved of Aton', but he was unable to restore order. After a short reign he vanished, giving way to Tutenkh-aton, who had married

Enkhosnepa-aton, 'She lives by the Aton', the third daughter of the reformer.

Tutenkh-aton was a boy when he ascended the throne, and for a time he endeavoured to support the religious reforms of his father-in-law, but he was not strong enough to resist the influence of the Theban priesthood. He was soon forced to give way, to abandon the new capital, to return to Thebes, and to restore the worship of Ammon, in token of which he changed his name to Tutenkh-amon. He reigned at least six years, but was only a youth at the time of his death in 1350 B.C. He was

FIG. 67. Iron dagger from the tomb of Tutenkh-amon.

succeeded by Aye, the priest, who had married the queen-mother Tiy, and both were over eighty years of age by this time. Their reign was short, for in a few months Harmhab, or Horemheb, the commander-in-chief of the army, though not of royal blood, led a revolt against these aged rulers, and in 1350 B.C. established himself on the throne as the first monarch of the 19th Dynasty.

It is believed that it was while Harmhab was marching on the capital that the few who remained faithful to the memory of Ikhn-aton embalmed the body of the deceased youth and buried it secretly with all the treasures of the family in the hillside in the Valley of the Kings. How this was discovered in 1922 by the patient search of Mr. Howard Carter and was opened by him and the late Earl of Carnarvon is fresh in the memory of all our readers. This is no place to describe the treasures found in this tomb, which have been very fully treated elsewhere. These treasures, though adding little to our knowledge of the obscure points in the history of the period, give a vivid idea of the wealth, luxury, and artistic skill of the time. One object only demands our attention here, for it is a harbinger of what was to come. In Tutenkh-amon's tomb was found an object, believed to have been of Hittite workmanship, adorned with gold; this, the earliest of its kind that has yet been discovered, was a knife or dagger of iron.

BOOKS

BREASTED, J. H. *A History of Egypt* (New York, 1912).
Cambridge Ancient History, vol. ii (Cambridge, 1924).
SMITH, SIDNEY. *Early History of Assyria* (London, 1928).
HALL, H. R. *Ancient History of the Near East* (London, 1913).

12

Chronological Summary

OUR summary of the events that took place during these centuries must be brief. We saw in *The Way of the Sea* that during the last phase of Hissarlik II, between 2200 and 1900 B.C., its inhabitants had been exploring central Europe, and had found copper in Slovakia and tin in the Erzgebirge, and had learned the art of making bronze, an alloy that had already long been known in Mesopotamia. We cannot date this opening up of Bohemia later than 2100 B.C., and about this time we find a metal culture arising in that area, known as the Marschwitz culture, in which tools of copper, sometimes containing a little tin, were used. No objects of true bronze, that is to say with about 10 per cent. of tin, have yet been found with this culture, for doubtless the men of Hissarlik kept the knowledge of the mixture a secret. About 2000 B.C., or perhaps slightly earlier, bronze implements, very like some found at Hissarlik, reached Portugal; other similar implements, and perhaps the knowledge of the alloy, arrived in the south of Spain about the same time. From these Iberian centres the new alloy spread rapidly along the Atlantic coast of Europe, and not long after 2000 B.C. had reached Brittany and the British Isles.

During the century following 2000 B.C. Egypt was flourishing under the rule of its 12th Dynasty, and the Cretan merchants, now in their Second Middle Minoan period, were carrying on a brisk trade with the people of the mouths of the Nile. The trade to the west remained for the most part in the hands of those Cycladic merchants who had settled at the head of the Gulf of Corinth, but our evidence suggests that the manufactured goods they carried came mostly from Hissarlik II, in whose interests, we believe, men came to the Iberian Peninsula in search of copper, tin, and gold. The beaker-makers still flourished in all the centres where they had made settlements, and seem to have had an organization for carrying goods, of Marschwitz and sometimes of Hissarlik manufacture, to those coastal settlements occupied by the builders of the megalithic monuments.

In central Germany a group of herdsmen, using cord-ornamented pottery, and coming originally, we believe, from the park-lands north of the Russian steppe, occupied the uplands and the plateau, where they buried their dead under mounds of earth. These will be called the Mound-builders. Towards the close of the century bronze became more commonly used by the Marschwitz people, whose culture was undergoing a change and passing into that known as Proto-Aunjetitz. At this time they seem to have passed under the rule of steppe-border leaders, perhaps of some of the Mound-builders, who were now spreading into south Germany.

In Britain we find the custom of erecting stone circles, perhaps copies of wooden circles like Woodhenge, which may have been introduced by immigrants from Holland. The Avebury circle seems to date from this time, and perhaps the earlier structure at Stonehenge. It was about this time that the deposits of alluvial gold were found in the Wicklow Hills in Ireland, and to this date, or perhaps a little later, we must attribute the jet necklaces, so often found in Scotland, and the gold crescents of Irish make that have a wide distribution in northwest Europe; it is possible, also, that certain gold torcs, one of which was found among the ruins of Hissarlik II, date from this century.

About 1900 B.C. the Second City of Hissarlik was attacked and burned, and with its fall its great commercial connexions came to an end. The organization of the beaker folk seems soon to have died out on the Continent, though their distinct culture survived for a time in Great Britain. Cut off from their source of supply of bronze implements, the Proto-Aunjetitz people developed a considerable industry for the manufacture of such goods, copying, for the most part, models that had reached them through the beaker organization, perhaps from Spain. This culture, which we may now call Aunjetitz, spread during this century into Silesia and west Poland, and, before its close, down the Oder valley; their bronze goods seem to have been carried into the surrounding regions. Another similar centre of activity, also dependent originally on influences from Hissarlik II, arose at Toszeg and Perjamos on the Tisza in Hungary, where the inhabitants obtained copper from the Slovakian Hills and gold from Transylvania. At Toszeg the people lived in a village, built on horizontal logs within a palisade of piles, and surrounded by a water-course. The Mound-builders spread into west Germany, and before the close of the century had reached the north-eastern parts of France.

Another centre for the manufacture of bronze arose about this time at El Argar in south-east Spain, and goods from here spread along the coast to the south of France, and thence through the Carcassonne Gap to the Bay of Biscay, thus reaching

Brittany and the British Isles. About this time, too, trade from El Argar passed across the south of France, along the 100-metre raised beach, crossed the Rhône above Avignon, and, traversing the Alps by the pass of Mt. Genèvre, reached the valley of the Po, and then, by means of the Brenner pass, the area of the Aunjetitz culture.

The fall of Hissarlik II removed a great rival to Cretan trade, which now began to expand to the west. The Cretans for this purpose dominated the activities of the Cycladic folk, and sent their goods by the old route from the Gulf of Corinth. Their influence had been felt from the first at El Argar, and by the roundabout way described in this and the preceding paragraph models of bronze axes and daggers, evolved in Crete, reached the Aunjetitz area and travelled as far north as the British Isles. During this century the Palace of Knossos was remodelled.

Shortly before 1900 B.C. fresh invaders reached Greece down the valley of the Spercheios; these may have been a southern branch-stream in an extensive movement of people towards the East, and it may have been another band of the same folk that destroyed Hissarlik II. These fresh arrivals in Greece, who seem to have been the Hellenes, settled round the Maliac Gulf and destroyed the Second City of Orchomenos and built the Third City on that site. They seem to have been the makers or users of Minyan ware. Soon after 1900 B.C. they seem to have raided some of the islands in the Aegean Sea, for their influence has been noted in Naxos and Syros, while the Second City of Phylakopi was fortified at this time as though its inhabitants feared an attack from outside. On the mound of Hissarlik a humble village arose, known as Hissarlik III.

About 1800 B.C. the rainfall, especially on the steppes and deserts, began to diminish, and various tribes from Syria and Palestine, feeling the drought, and perhaps also disturbed by the arrival of Hittites and Kharrians in North Syria, began to settle in the eastern part of the Delta. This created trouble in Egypt, and in 1788 B.C. the 12th Dynasty came to an end. The rule of the 13th Dynasty was not strong enough to prevent the intruders from spreading, and, though they succeeded in keeping alive some kind of government, prosperity in Egypt declined. It was probably towards the close of this century that Joseph arrived in Egypt. In 1766 B.C. the Kassites, a tribe of hillmen from the Zagros Mountains, conquered Babylon, where Gandash set himself up as first king of the Second Dynasty, and before the end of the century his successor had conquered the Sea Country.

This unsettled state in Egypt paralysed trade with Crete, whose merchants sought fresh markets and increased their commerce with Sicily, South Italy, and Spain. This trade flourished until the latter half of the century, when it began to decline, probably because the readily worked tin-bearing sands were beginning to be exhausted, and it became necessary to go farther afield for fresh supplies. Towards the end of the century the Cretan populace seems to have revolted against its lords, and the palaces of Knossos and Phaestos were burned. The revolt seems to have resulted in the rise of a new dynasty; the palaces were rebuilt and Crete entered its Third Middle Minoan period. Another village, Hissarlik IV, succeeded Hissarlik III. In 1766 B.C., according to legendary history, T'ang overthrew Chieh Kwei, the wicked emperor of China, bringing the Hsia Dynasty to an end, and ascended the throne as first emperor of the Shang or Yin Dynasty.

The Aunjetitz culture spread along the loess and into the Elster-Saale-Elbe region, where there were rich deposits of salt, also into west Moravia, where it mingled with elements coming from Toszeg and Perjamos; bronze implements of Aunjetitz manufacture were carried into Lower Austria, and up the Inn valley and across the Brenner Pass into north Italy, where they were used in the pile-dwellings at the margins of the lakes. The

Mound-builders extended their range into the valley of the Saône and passed down the valley of the Rhône as far as Vienne.

About 1700 B.C. the Hyksos had conquered most of Egypt, and the 13th Dynasty came to an end in 1690 B.C., when a local chief established the 14th Dynasty at Thebes. The Hyksos rulers were considered the 15th Dynasty, and towards the middle of the century another line of these invaders set up the 16th Dynasty. Crete had now, as already stated, entered its Third Middle Minoan period, the golden age of its existence, in spite of the fact that during most of the century all trade with Egypt had ceased. It was at this time that a linear script, apparently of syllabic type, superseded the hieroglyphs formerly in use here. The Hellenes continued to expand throughout Greece. They destroyed the Second City of Lianokladhi about 1650 B.C. and rebuilt it; they then penetrated most of the Peloponnese.

Early in this century the Dardanians, a hill tribe from Macedonia, invaded Asia Minor; they built a city on the mound at Hissarlik, known as Hissarlik V. New settlements, somewhat similar to those that had been destroyed, arose in the Black Earth Lands of south Russia, and this culture, with its painted pottery, spread across Galicia almost as far west as Breslau.

The Aunjetitz culture continued to flourish and spread in central Europe, and some of its bronze implements were carried from the Italian lakes across the Alps to the lake-dwellings in Switzerland, while a new type of axe-head, with flanges on its sides, spread through the Po valley into the south of France, and through the Carcassonne Gap to the Atlantic coast, and thence northwards as far as Britain. The Mound-builders continued to spread, and during this century reached the west of Hungary.

About the beginning of this century a group of steppe folk living in Turkistan in the region around Balkh were driven by drought to change their quarters and to settle near Nisaya. Later on they divided into two groups, the first of which settled at Kabul and the other at Herat. The Shang emperors enlarged their dominions until they reached the neighbourhood of Peking and extended to the south of the Yangtse.

About 1625 B.C. some of the Cretans settled in the Peloponnese and founded cities at Tiryns and Mycenae, where they made themselves masters of a mixed population, which contained Hellenic elements. In 1620 B.C. Sekenenre I, a king of the 17th Dynasty at Thebes, began to drive the Hyksos out, a process which was continued by his son and his grandson of the same name.

By 1600 B.C. the Hyksos had been expelled from the greater part of Egypt, and by 1580 B.C. Ahmose, the son and successor of Sekenenre III, finally drove them out of the country and established himself as the first king of the 18th Dynasty. His son Amenhotep I pursued them into Asia in 1557 B.C. and conquered the country as far as the Euphrates. Thutmose I, who succeeded him in 1540 B.C., consolidated this Asiatic empire and defeated the Mitanni. He died in 1514 B.C., when he was succeeded by his only daughter, Hatshepsut, who married and ruled jointly with Thutmose II.

At the beginning of this century the Palaces of Knossos and Phaestos were destroyed by fire, probably the result of an earthquake; all the palaces and villas were immediately restored, and Knossos became the capital of the island. With this restoration Crete entered its First Late Minoan period and trade was resumed with Egypt. In the Peloponnese, Mycenae became the main seat of Cretan power, and from there the Cretan princes governed their other cities of Tiryns, Corinth, and the two known as Pylos. Towards the close of the century the princes of Mycenae evidently feared attack from without, for the city was strongly fortified.

Direct communication with the West had ceased apparently when the tin-sands of Spain and Portugal had been exhausted, but the countries on the Atlantic continued to evolve a bronze culture of their own. In Spain the halberd had been developed from the dagger, and simple spear-heads had come into use. These were developed in Britain by the addition of a ring to prevent the haft from splitting, and soon the socketed spearhead was evolved and passed through a number of experimental stages. In course of time a stop-ridge appeared between the flanges of the axe-head and soon became the well-known palstave, which quickly spread in Germany, Britain, western France and ultimately Portugal.

The settlements on the Tisza continued to flourish, and their culture crossed the Carpathians into Little Poland and then to Silesia, where it came into contact with the Aunjetitz culture, The result of this combination was to produce a new culture. known as that of Lausitz, which soon dominated large parts of central Europe. The civilization of the Tisza passed up the Danube to South Germany and Switzerland, and large numbers of people from Hungary passed round the head of the Adriatic to the valley of the Po, where they founded what are known as the *Terremare*. The steppe tribes, who had settled at Herat, seem to have become divided owing to a religious controversy, and while one group remained in Persia the other migrated eastwards in the direction of India.

In 1501 B.C. Thutmose II died and Hatshepsut married Thutmose III, but still remained the predominant partner. She organized a great expedition to Punt and reopened the copper mines in the Wadi Maghara. She retained her Asiatic empire without sending an army there. She died in 1479 B.C., and the same year the king of Kadesh organized a revolt in Asia. Thutmose III led an army to quell it, and these warlike expeditions became an annual feature of his subsequent reign. In

1448 B.C. he associated his son Amenhotep with him on the throne, and died the next year. Scarcely had Amenhotep II gained sole power when the Syrians started a revolt, and he led two expeditions to put it down. At his death, in 1420 B.C., he was succeeded by Thutmose IV who, like his predecessors, had to quell a revolt in Syria; he formed an alliance with the Mitanni, and married the daughter of Artatama their king. He died in 1411 B.C., when he was succeeded by Amenhotep III. Of the Kassite kings of Babylon we learn little during this century, but the Hittites were increasing in power and threatening the Asiatic possessions of Egypt.

In Crete the power of Knossos increased and the island entered its Second Late Minoan period. To this time some attribute the legends of Minos the law-giver. A new dynasty seems to have arisen at Mycenae, and it appears probable that some Hellenic adventurers had overthrown the Cretan prince who was ruling there. A fresh Cretan settlement was made at Thebes, an echo of which has come down in the story of Cadmus. The Fourth City arose at Orchomenos, and its inhabitants drained the Lake Copais, while the Cretans established an oracle at Delphi.

Western and central Europe continued to develop their own bronze culture. Prosperity declined in Spain, but bronze palstaves continued in general use in north Germany, while the Lausitz culture flourished farther south. The village of Toszeg declined, for many of its inhabitants had departed to found the *terremare* of the Po valley. A dry and warm period seems to have set in throughout central Europe, the glaciers melted more rapidly, and the levels of the lakes rose. The steppe folk who, owing to religious differences, had left their companions at Herat, descended into the Punjab as the Aryan invaders of India.

Soon after 1400 B.C. the Amurru plundered Syria, and

shortly afterwards desert tribes, who appear to have been the Hebrews under Joshua, crossed the Jordan into Palestine. Amenhotep III sent over an army to restore order, but the Asiatic empire of Egypt was in a precarious condition when he died in 1375 B.C. His son, Amenhotep IV, started a new religion and changed his name to Ikhn-aton, and, since he apparently neglected the affairs of state, his empire in Asia had all disappeared at the time of his death in 1358 B.C. About the same time the Hittites invaded the territory of the Mitanni.

About 1400 B.C. the Palace of Knossos and all the other palaces and villas in Crete were destroyed. This is thought to have been the result of an invasion, some account of which has survived in the story of Theseus. Crete now entered its Third Late Minoan period. The walls of Hissarlik were rebuilt, and the Sixth City, Homer's Troy, was founded. After the death of Ikhn-aton first one son-in-law and then another succeeded to the throne; the second of these was Tutenkh-aton. He soon restored the old religion and changed his name to Tutenkh-amon, but died in 1350 B.C., when his wife's grandmother Tiy and her husband Aye ascended the throne. They died the same year, when Horemheb, the commander-in-chief of the army, ascended the throne as first monarch of the 19th Dynasty. Many great treasures were discovered in the tomb of Tutenkh-amon, and among them a dagger with a hilt of gold but a blade of iron.

INDEX

Names of countries, rivers, lakes, seas, mountains, and names quoted to describe the situations of places, have been omitted to shorten the index.

Aah-hotep 123
Abd-Ashirta 152
Abingdon 62
Adlerberg 49
Aegisthus, Treasury of 106
Agni 125
Agum 114, 116, 141
Ahmose 122, 123, 142, 144, 163
Ahriman 126, 154
Ahura-Mazda 126, 154
Akhet-Aton 154
Akhn-aton see Ikhn-aton
Alderley Edge 22
Aleppo 116, 148
Alexandria 86
Almaden 26
Alpine race 7, 8, 113
Amarna 155
Ambala 131   [152, 163, 166
Amenhotep 141, 144, 148–50,
Amesbury 33
Ammon 153, 154, 156
Amurru 148, 152, 165
Anyang 138
Apopi 122
Arachosia 129, 130
Arahvaiti 129, 130
Arbor Low 36
Argolis 90, 94, 106
Arles 73
Arreton Down 79, 80
Artashumana 142
Artatama 142, 149, 150, 165
Ashur-bel-nisheshu 141
Ashur-nadin-akhi 141
Ashur-nirari 141
Ashur-rabi 141
Ashur-rin-nisheshu 141
Askabad 129, 130
Aton 153
Atreus, Treasury of 106, 107
Aunjetitz culture 9, 41, 50, 60, 64, 74, 78, 159–64
Avaris 118, 123
Avebury 36, 38, 158
Avesta 125, 127, 128, 130
Avignon 160
Aye 152, 154, 156, 166
Aziru 152

Badarians 133, 134
Bakhdi 129, 130
Balearic Islands 72
Balkh 128–30, 162
Barvas 36
Batu 134
Bayeux 77   [159
Beaker type 4, 6, 7, 42, 158,
Belfort, pass of 77
Beth-pelet 118, 119
Bilce Złota 66
Bleasdale 32, 38
Boeotia 106
Boghaz Keui 141, 151
Bouchier, G. 127

Brahmans 124, 131, 135
Brenner pass 64, 160, 161
Breslau 46, 162
Brno (Brünn) 46
Bryn Celli Du 28, 29
Burna-Buriash 114, 141
Butmir 111
Cabut 19
Cadmus 109, 165
Cairo 118
Callernish 36
Carcassonne Gap 159, 162
Carchemish 116, 144, 148
Caria 88
Carmel, Mt. 147
Carnac 28, 29, 32, 37
Cassiterides 20
Castellazzo 67, 69
Cas Tor 32
Chalcis 109
Channel Islands 11, 78
Chieh Kwei 137, 161
Ch'öng-T'ang 137
Chou 137, 140
Chou-sin 138, 139
Ch'ung, Marquis of 140
Clytemnestra, Treasury of 106
Coffey, G. 22
Col de Tende 52
Collorgues 73
Copais, L. 109, 165
Crissa 109
Cucuteni 66

Damascus 152
Dardanelles 93
Dardanians 111, 162
Dasas or Dasyus 137
Déchelette, J. 53, 76
Delphi 109, 165
Delta 117, 118, 144, 146, 161
Der el-Bahri 145
Dhimini 93
Dongola 149
Dublin 24
Dudkhalis 116, 141
Dyaus 125

Ea-gamil 114
Ecbatana 126, 129
Elam 113, 148
El Argar 11–16, 91, 159, 160
Enkhosnepa-aton 156
Enlil-nasir 141
Erdeven 30
Eriba-Adad 141
Er Lannic 32
Erzgebirge 41, 42, 78, 157
Etel 30, 37
Euboea 92, 94, 109
Evans, Sir Arthur 87, 104, 106
Eye see Aye

Fa 140
Fauvillers 24
Fiume 107
Fuente Alamo 91

Gandash 114, 161
Gaza 147
Gilukhipa 150
Glatz 42, 46
Glotz, G. 86
Goshen 119
Gournia 96
Grunty Fen 24
Gu 113
Gushtasp see Vistasp
Habiru 152
Hagia Triada 88, 98
Hammurabi 114
Hannover 24
Hapta-Hindu 129, 130
Harappa 136
Harendermolen 38
Harlyn Bay 22, 24
Harmhab see Horemheb
Haroyu 129, 130
Harran 120
Hatshepsut 144–7, 163, 164
Hattushil 141
Hebrides 36, 78
Hellas 93
Helmand 129, 130
Hengistbury 33
Herakles 111
Herat 129, 130, 163–5
Homer 166
Horemheb 156, 166
Hradek 46
Hsia dynasty 57, 137, 161
Hsiao Tun Tsun 138
Ikhn-aton 153, 155, 166
Indra 125
Intef 117
Ishme-Dagon 141
Isle of Man 78
Isopata 101

Jordan 166
Joseph 119–21, 161
Josephus 119, 120
Joshua 152, 166

Kabul 129, 130, 131, 163
Kadashman-Enlil 141
Kadesh 147, 148, 164
Kadi Keui 25
Kadmeia 109
Kamares ware 82
Kamose 123
Kantara 147
Kara-indash 141
Karnak 146, 148
Kashtiliash 114
Katna 152
Keftiu 101
Kerlescant 30
Kermario 30, 32
Kharians 114, 116–8, 141, 160
Khian 90, 121, 123
Kish 1
Kishman 128
Kudurru 115

Index

Kurigalsu 141
Lagozza 55
Laomedon 111
Lausitz 60, 61, 64, 164, 165
Lesnewth 23, 24
Les Roseaux 54
Levkas 94
Lianokladi 94, 111, 162
Ligures 53, 68
Linz 107
Ljubljana (Laibach) 66
Llanbedr 28
Llanllyfni 23
Long Meg 36
Los Millares 16
Lycia 88
Maliac Gulf 92, 93, 160
Malik-Arakh 116
Mallia 96
Malta 28, 86, 91
Manetho 118
Manio 30
Mantua 68
March 41
Margiana 129, 130   [158
Marschwitz 42, 45, 46, 49, 157,
Matera 72
Mediterranean race 8, 136
Megiddo 147
Meli-shipak 141
Melos 100
Memphis 118, 149, 154
Ménec 30–32
Mercurago 55
Merit-aton 155
Merivale Bridge 32
Merv 129, 130
Milocca 71
Minos 88, 101–3, 112, 165
Minotaur 102   [111, 160
Minyan ware 93, 94, 104, 108,
Mitra 125
Mochlos 88
Mohenjo-daro 136
Montale 69
Montelius 50, 75
Morges 54
Much, M. 22
Müller, Max 131
Mura 129, 130
Mursilis 116
Mutemuya 150
Nal 136, 137
Napata 149
Nasa 129, 130
Nauplia 106
Nâvsâri 126
Naxos 92, 94, 160
Nazi-Maruttash 141
Nefer-tete 152
Nehavend 126, 129
New Grange 27, 28
Nippur 114
Nisa 129, 130
Nisaya 129, 130, 163
Nishapur 129, 130

Nordic race 8, 10, 113–4, 118, 123
Olomouc (Olmütz) 46
Ophrys 96   [165
Orchomenos 93, 96, 109, 160
Ouranos 125
Pagasaic Gulf 109
Palaikastro 96
Parc-er-Guren 19
Parsis 124–7
Parthians 114
Pelusium 118
Peking 137, 163
Penrith 36
Penzance 23, 24
Perjamos 42, 159, 161
Persepolis 127, 129
Peschiera 55
Petrie, Sir Flinders 117, 118
Phaestos 81, 82, 90, 96, 161, 163
Pharos 86
Phocis 93
Phylakopi 92, 160
Pigorini, L. 67
Pileta Cave 26
Plemmirio 71
Plymstock 79
Port Said 118
Pouy de la Halliade 73   [7
Predmost-Combe Capelle type
Priam 112   [159
Proto-Aunjetitz phase 44, 158,
Pseira 96
Punt 147, 164
Puzur-ashur 141
Pylos 106, 163
Rekmere 100
Rhaga 129, 130
Reche, O. 6
Rig-Veda 124–6, 128, 131
Rimi-Malek 116
Rouzic, Z. le 11, 19
Sai-ma Ts'ien 139
St. David's 22
St. Germain 37   [71
Santiago da Compostella 23,
Sargon 113, 117
Saronic Gulf 96, 102
Scythians 66
Sekenenre 122, 123, 163
Senekhtenre 123
Shahnama 131
Shang dynasty 137–9, 161, 163
Shap 32
Sharuhen 118, 123
Shaushshatar 142
Shubad Q. 13, 44
Shubbiluliuma 141, 155
Shuttarna 142, 150
Sinai 117, 147
Siret, L. 14, 20
Spitâma 126
Stennis 36   [159
Stonehenge 29, 33–8, 40, 158,
Straubing 46, 50
Su 113, 138

Subaraeans 116, 136, 151
Sughda 129, 130
Sumerians 116, 136, 151
Surât 126, 127
Susa 136
Syracuse 71
Syros 92, 94, 160
Tadukhipa 150
Ta-ki 138, 139
T'ang 137, 138, 161
Taranto 68
Telibinus 116
Tell-el-Amarna 151, 154
Tell-el-Yehudiyeh 118   [165
Terremare 58, 66–9, 70, 164,
Tharu 147
Thisbe 106
Thutmose 100, 144–50, 155, 163, 164   [163
Tiryns 90, 94, 102, 106, 112,
Tiy Q. 152, 154, 156, 166
Toszeg 42–3, 58, 159, 161, 165
Triphylia 106
Tripolje 66
Troezen 102
Troy 53, 112, 166
Turanians 128, 131
Turks 82   [155
Tushratta 142, 143, 150, 152,
Tutenkh-amon 155–7, 166
Tutenkh-aton see Tutenkh-amon
Tylissos 96
Ula-Buriash 114
Unetiče see Aunjetitz
Ur 13, 44, 53, 120
Urumya 128, 129
Urva 129, 130
Vaekereta 129, 130
Vapheio 88, 90, 91, 106
Varena 129, 130
Varuna 125
Vedas see Rig-Veda
Veddas 134
Vehr-Kana 129, 130
Vienna 107
Vinelz 53
Vistasp 128, 130
Vouga, P. 53
Wadi Maghara 147, 164
Wadi Tumilat 146
Warrington 20
Weinzierl 45
Windmill Hill 36
Wön-wang 139, 140
Woodhenge 32, 38–40
Wu-wang 140
Yin dynasty see Shang
Ysbyty Cynfyn 37, 38
Yu 137
Yu-li 140
Zafer Papoura 101, 108
Zagazig 118
Zakro 96
Zarathustra see Zoroaster
Zoroaster 127, 128, 130, 154

/571P313V.7>C1/

Date Due

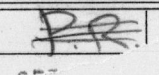